Contents

KT-460-820

Introduction   iv

Chapter One   The development of the European Union   1
Chapter Two   Joining the EU   9
Chapter Three   The EU and national governments   23
Chapter Four   Producing in the EU   48
Chapter Five   Working in the EU   62
Chapter Six   Farming in the EU   78
Chapter Seven   The EU, trade and the global economy   93

Examination skills for The European Union   113
Conclusion   120
Index   121

Introduction

This is a completely new edition of *The European Union*. The book examines some of the key issues facing consumers, producers, workers and governments of the EU today. It explores the future of the EU, how EU policies affect national economies and how globalisation is influencing the EU.

This book is designed to cover the requirements of Module 2888 of Economics in a European Context, AQA's Module 4 'Working as an Economist' and Edexcel's Unit 6 'The UK in a Global Context'. It does, however, have a wider coverage. This is because, while the concepts and issues are discussed in an EU context, the emphasis is on the economics rather than on institutions. The concepts and issues can be applied in a range of contexts. Indeed, the book should prove useful for students studying not only A level economics, but also those studying AS level, HND and degree courses.

Chapter 1 provides some brief, historical background to the EU, and distinguishes between different types of economic blocs. In Chapter 2 the criteria that countries joining the EU have to meet is examined. The impact of EU enlargement is also analysed from the point of view of both the new members and the established members. Chapter 3 focuses on a range of EU policies including the single currency, the Growth and Stability Pact, transport policies, and the EU budget.

In Chapter 4, attention moves to the impact of the single market and the challenges and opportunities facing producers in the EU. Chapter 5 switches from producers to workers. Among the topics covered in this chapter are the causes of unemployment in the EU, the advantages and disadvantages of flexible labour markets, working hours and working conditions, minimum wages, migration and differences between European labour market models.

Chapter 6 explores why agriculture is protected, the volatility of agricultural markets and an assessment of the effectiveness of the CAP. Chapter 7 explores trade between EU member countries, trade between the EU and the rest of the world, and how globalisation is influencing the EU. The new Examination skills section gives guidance suitable for all boards. It includes how to decipher questions, answering data response questions, and how to avoid some common pitfalls.

The European Union

Fifth Edition

Susan Grant
Abingdon and Witney College

Colin G. Bamford
University of Huddersfield

Series editor: Susan Grant

www.heinemann.co.uk
✓ Free online support
✓ Useful weblinks
✓ 24 hour online ordering

01865 888058

EG37417

Heinemann Educational Publishers
Halley Court, Jordan Hill, Oxford OX2 8EJ
Part of Harcourt Education

Heinemann is a registered trademark of Harcourt Education Limited

© Colin Bamford and Sue Grant, 2006

First published 2006

10 09 08 07
10 9 8 7 6 5 4 3 2

British Library Cataloguing in Publication Data is available
from the British Library on request.

ISBN: 978 0 435 332 35 8

Edited by Kathy Peltan
Designed by Peter Stratton
Typeset and Illustrated by TechType

Original illustrations © Harcourt Education Limited, 2006
Cover design by Peter Stratton

Printed in the UK by Ashford Colour Press Ltd
Picture research by Jemma Street

[1 1 MAR 2010]

Acknowledgements
Colin Bamford would like to thank Katie Barrett for help in word processing the manuscript.
Every effort has been made to contact copyright holders of material reproduced in this book. Any
omissions will be rectified in subsequent printings if notice is given to the publishers.

Photo acknowledgements: Bettmann/Corbis page 6; Régis Bossu/Sygma/Corbis page 55; AP Photo/
Jacques Brinon/Empics page 74; Raymond Gehman/Corbis page 88.

1 The development of the European Union

In this chapter you will learn:

- how the nature of the EU has changed over time
- what is the difference between free trade areas, customs unions, common markets, and economic and monetary unions
- how the EU has grown over time
- what are the roles of the key EU institutions.

> **Key words** common market • customs union
> the European Economic Area • the European Free Trade Association
> the European Union • eurozone • free trade area
> new member states

Introduction

The world is increasingly developing into one market place. This process of national boundaries being broken down, and national economies becoming more integrated, can be seen in the context of the development of the **European Union** (EU). During its existence, the EU has seen changes to its name, nature, membership and relationship with non-member countries. Its institutions have evolved with these changes.

Origins and names

The origins of what has become known as the EU go back to the ending of the Second World War. This war had resulted in an extensive loss of life and property in Europe. A number of leading politicians and economists blamed the war on aggressive nationalism. They believed that further conflict could be avoided by greater integration of European economies. One politician who argued for greater cooperation between European countries and greater coordination of their economic policies was Jean Monnet. This French politician, known as the 'father of European integration', led the European movement in the 1950s and 1960s. His ultimate vision was full economic and political union with a 'United States of Europe'.

The first stages towards European integration were the formation of the European Coal and Steel Community (ECSC) in 1952 and the European Atomic Energy Community (Euratom) in 1957. The ECSC created a **free trade area** in coal and steel, regarded at the time as two key industries, between member countries, protection against non-members and a supranational body to take council decisions on pricing and production. Euratom sought to encourage the growth of nuclear industries, promoted research and development in nuclear power and into the peaceful use of nuclear energy.

The members of the ECSC and Euratom were Belgium, France, Germany, Italy, Luxembourg and West Germany. The economic bloc we now know as the EU came into existence with the signing the Treaty of Rome in 1957. It consisted of Belgium, France, Germany, Italy, Luxembourg, West Germany and the Netherlands. It came into formal existence under the name of the European Economic Community (EEC) on 1 January 1958. Nine years later, in 1967, the name was changed to the European Community (EC). Then in 1992 it became the European Union. We will refer to the EU throughout this book, even if we are discussing a time when it was the EC or EEC.

Economic blocs

The nature of the economic blocs that countries can form differ in the degree of their integration. The changes in the name of the EU reflect the greater integration of member states which has occurred over its existence. There are four main types of economic bloc.

A free trade area

This involves a limited degree of integration. The member countries agree to remove restrictions on trade between each other, while being permitted to maintain their own individual restrictions on products from non-members. An example of a free trade area is the **European Free Trade Association** (EFTA). This was based on a proposal by the UK and was formed in 1960. Its original members were Austria, Denmark, Norway, Portugal, Sweden, Switzerland and the UK. Over time, five countries left to join the EU and two new countries joined. EFTA now consists of Iceland, Liechtenstein, Norway and Switzerland. EFTA has free trade in manufactured goods. Agriculture, however, is not covered.

NAFTA (North American Free Trade Association), which compromises Canada, Mexico and the USA is also, as its name suggests, a free trade area. NAFTA and the EU are the two most powerful economic blocs in the world.

A customs union

This goes a stage further in integration. As well as having free trade between member countries, there is also a common external trade policy. Member countries place the same trade restrictions on non-member countries' products. The EU started life as a **customs union**, with member countries being required to impose a common external tariff (CET). Another example of a customs union, or rather an economic bloc moving towards being a customs union, is Mercosur. This has developed out of the Latin American Free Trade Association. It became a partial customs union in 1995 when the members, Argentina, Brazil, Paraguay and Uruguay, imposed a CET covering 85 per cent of products exported. The Southern African Customs Union (SACU) also operates a common external tariff.

Common, or single, market

In this case, as well as having free movements of products and a CET, there is also free movement of capital and labour between member countries. This should generate greater competitive pressure which, in turn, can increase economic efficiency. It also involves a greater need to coordinate policies between member states. The Single European Act (SEM) 1986 increased the degree of integration in the EU by seeking to remove all barriers to the free movement of products, people and capital, and thereby creating a single European market. Caricom (the Caribbean Community), including the Bahamas, Barbados, Jamaica, Trinidad and Tobago, and nine other countries, also has aspects of a **common market**.

Economic and monetary union (EMU)

This involves the highest degree of integration. With full EMU, as well as operating a single market, member countries have the same currency and pursue the same economic policies. The Single European Act committed the EU to move towards EMU. It has made some progress towards this with the adoption of the single currency, the euro. There is, however, debate as to the extent to which there should be further integration.

The European Economic Area (EEA)

In 1992, the EU signed an agreement with the members of the EFTA to form the EEA, which took effect two years later. The EU extended its single market with its free movement of goods, services, capital and people to the EFTA states and in return the EFTA states agreed to accept many of the laws and regulations of the EU, and to make a small contribution to the EU budget.

Some areas, however, are not covered by the agreement. These include agriculture, defence, the **eurozone**, fisheries and foreign policy.

Switzerland actually rejected EEA membership in 1993, so the EEA currently consists of the EU members plus Iceland, Norway and Liechtenstein.

Membership

The number of members of the EU has grown over time from its original six and is set to continue to grow. Table 1 shows that the most significant increase, in terms of addition to GDP, occurred in 1973 while the largest increase, in terms of number of countries, took place in 2004.

Table 1.1: The enlargement of the EU

Enlargement date	Countries joining	Population % addition	GDP % addition	GDP per head entrants as a % of existing average
1973	Denmark, Ireland & UK	33.4	31.9	95.5
1981	Greece	3.7	1.8	48.4
1988	Portugal & Spain	17.8	11.0	62.2
1995	Austria, Finland & Sweden	6.3	6.5	103.6
2004	Cyprus, Czech Republic, Estonia, Latvia, Hungary, Lithuania, Malta, Poland, Slovakia & Slovenia	19.6	9.1	46.5

Figure 1.1 shows the countries currently in the EU and four of those awaiting entry. Among the members of the EU there are a number of different groupings. A current common division is between what is called the EU15 (those countries which had become members by 1995) and the **new member states** (NMS). The NMS joined in 2004 and are sometimes also referred to as the EU10. The NMS8 are the NMS minus Cyprus and Malta, and are all former planned economies. Cyprus and Malta are relatively small countries and were not former planned economies.

There is also a division between those countries that have adopted the single currency and those that have not. The former group is referred to, collectively, as the eurozone, euro area, euroland or EU12. In 2006 the members of the eurozone were Austria, Belgium, Finland, France, Germany,

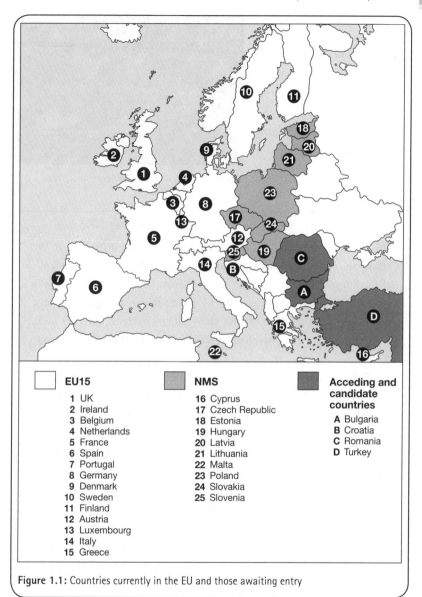

Figure 1.1: Countries currently in the EU and those awaiting entry

EU15

1 UK
2 Ireland
3 Belgium
4 Netherlands
5 France
6 Spain
7 Portugal
8 Germany
9 Denmark
10 Sweden
11 Finland
12 Austria
13 Luxembourg
14 Italy
15 Greece

NMS

16 Cyprus
17 Czech Republic
18 Estonia
19 Hungary
20 Latvia
21 Lithuania
22 Malta
23 Poland
24 Slovakia
25 Slovenia

Acceding and candidate countries

A Bulgaria
B Croatia
C Romania
D Turkey

Greece, Ireland, Italy, Luxembourg, Netherlands, Portugal and Spain. The NMS are expected to join relatively soon (see Chapter 2).

In addition, EU member countries can be grouped according to income levels, influence and objectives. For instance, some economists refer to the EU3. This group, which consists of France, Germany and the UK, includes the three largest EU economies. The EU5 is the EU3 plus Italy and Spain.

Distinctions can also be made between members on the basis of their views of the future direction of the EU. For example, while France favours high EU spending on agriculture and further integration, the UK is pressing for reducing spending on agriculture and a lower degree of further integration.

Figure 1.2: The UK signs the Accession to the European Union in 1973

Key institutions

There are a number of key institutions in the EU, including these four.

- The European Council (EC). This is the most powerful institution in the EU. It consists of the leaders of each member state, plus the President of the European Commission. It meets at least twice a year, but usually more often. At these meetings, the EC makes major strategic decisions, such as deciding on the terms for enlargement, agreeing the EU's budget, reforming policy and providing guidelines for the future development of the EU.

- The European Commission. What the EC decides, the European Commission implements. It manages the EU budget, checks that the provisions of the EU treaties are carried out and represents the EU at meetings of the WTO (World Trade Organization). It is, however, rather more than just an administrative body. It drives integration and, as well as proposing legislation to the EC and mediating between national governments to achieve agreement on legislation, it directly legislates on issues that relate to agriculture, competition and trade.

- The Council of Ministers. The Council of Ministers is the EU's main legislative body. It does not have a fixed membership. What determines the membership is the issue under review. For instance, if transport is being considered, national ministers of transport will meet.

- The European Central Bank (ECB). The ECB operates monetary policy in the eurozone. Its principal task is to achieve price stability. This has been defined as an increase in HICP (harmonised index of consumer prices) of less than 2 per cent. If it believes there is a risk of inflation rising above 2 per cent, it will increase the rate of interest. It will also influence the value of the euro if it is considered necessary, holds foreign reserves, and issues euro notes and cent coins.

Summary

In this chapter you have learned that:

- one of the key aims of the EU, from its start, has been to preserve peace in Europe
- the EU has always been more than a free trade area; it started as a customs union, developed into a common market and is moving towards economic and monetary union
- the EU has joined with the EFTA to form the EEA
- membership of the EU grew from six to 25 members in 2004, and is set to grow further in the future
- the ECB operates monetary policy in the eurozone.

Further reading

Grant, S., Vidler, C., Section 4.2 in *Heinemann Economics A2 for AQA*, Heinemann, 2003

Grant, S., Vidler, C., Section 6.1 in *Heinemann Economics for OCR*, Heinemann, 2003

Griffiths, A., Wall, S., Chapters 28 and 29 in *Economics: Applied Economics* (10th edition), Prentice Hall, 2004

Useful websites

History of the EU: www.let.leidenuniv.nl/history/rtg/rel/index.htm

EU and the UK: www.cec.org.uk/index.htm

EU: www.europa.eu.int/index_en.htm

Activities

Topics for investigation

Using current newspaper articles and editorials, assess the views of the main UK political parties on the future direction of the EU.

Exam-style practice questions

Data response question

Economic blocs – moving forward?

Over time, economic blocs can become more or less integrated. The EU is currently moving towards economic and monetary union.

Mercosur is not as integrated as the EU. It is moving towards becoming a customs union. Commentators, however, have claimed that it is constructing an 'imperfect customs union'. There are nearly 800 exceptions to its common external tariff, including cars and sugar. In 2004, Argentina placed tariffs on Brazilian televisions, shoes and other goods. This infuriated Brazil, which also placed the blame for the EU's reluctance to open its agricultural market to Mercosur on Argentina's protectionism. Brazil is keen to develop links with the EU, which is one of its main trading partners. Argentina, in turn, criticises Brazil for not recognising all of its partners' food-quality standards and for subsidising its own exports. Brazil has also only ratified just over half of Mercosur resolutions.

The future of Mercosur is uncertain. In fact, it could go in one of three directions. It may stop trying to be a customs union and settle for being a free trade area. It could continue as a customs union, albeit a partial one. Alternatively it may develop into a common market.

1. Define:
   a) a 'common external tariff'   (2)
   b) 'protectionism'.   (2)
2. Comment on the extent to which Mercosur is a customs union.   (7)
3. Explain one advantage to an economy of being a member of a common market.   (6)
4. Discuss the advantages to the EU of its developing closer links with Mercosur.   (8)

2 Joining the EU

In this chapter you will learn:
- the criteria countries have to meet to join the EU
- why convergence and integration are important
- why countries want to join the EU
- how countries prepare for EU membership
- what are the initial stages of membership
- how the entry of ten new member states in 2004 has affected both the new members and the EU15
- how the EU may be enlarged in the future.

> **Key words** *acquis communautaire* • convergence
> Copenhagen criteria • economies of scale • flat taxes
> foreign direct investment • integration • the single currency
> trade creation • trade diversion

Introduction

What has now become the European Union began with only six member countries. Within 47 years, its membership had grown to 25. The growth of EU membership has not finished. More countries are seeking to join, hoping that membership will improve their economic performance. However, the impact that membership can have on a country's economy varies. Some economies appear to be transformed after entry. Other countries seem to struggle to take advantage of the opportunities and to respond to the challenges that membership brings.

The entry of new countries not only affects their economies, but also the economies of established members. Again the impact can vary, influenced in part by how similar the new members are when they join, and how they respond to being in the EU.

Criteria for joining

The most fundamental condition that any country has to meet is that it is in Europe! This is set down in the 1991 Maastricht Treaty (also known as the Treaty on European Union). Since 1993 there have also been four other conditions. Three of these are known as the **Copenhagen criteria**, as they were set out during a meeting of the European Council in Copenhagen in 1993. Any European country wishing to join the EU has to:

- have a functioning market economy and the capacity to cope with competitive pressures
- have a stable democracy; this includes having a multi-party parliament, respect for the rule of law, human rights and minorities, good neighbourly relations and no territorial disputes
- accept, implement and enforce the *acquis communautaire*, i.e. the whole body of the established laws, policies and rules. It consists of about 85 000 pages of EU legislation and regulation.

The fourth condition is that now any new member has to join the single currency (see Chapter 3).

Convergence and integration

The impact on new members coming into the EU and the impact on established members depends significantly on the degree of **convergence** and **integration** that occurs before and after membership.

There are two types of convergence – cyclical and structural. Cyclical convergence occurs when economies are operating at the same stage of the economic cycle. Structural convergence takes place when economies have similar economic structures and institutions. The more a new member's economy converges with established members, the more likely it is that the new member will benefit from common policies, and the easier it is to design EU-wide policies.

Integration involves economies working more as one. Achieving this requires not only the removal of barriers to the free movement of products and resources, but also the adoption of similar economic policies.

Why do countries want to join the EU?

Countries want to join the EU because they believe it will bring them both political and economic benefits. Working closely with other European countries tends to reduce conflicts, generate greater internal political stability and give greater international political influence.

Their governments also think it will strengthen their economies in a number of ways. Being able to sell to the world's largest single market without any barriers could enable their businesses to produce on a large scale. If this occurs, their businesses should be able to lower their average costs by reaping a range of **economies of scale**.

Industries and regions are also likely to benefit from access to EU funding in the form of CAP (Common Agricultural Policy) subsidies and regional spending. It was estimated, for instance, that the NMS economies were boosted by €14 billion in EU funds each in the period 2004 to 2006.

There are other reasons why economic growth and general economic performance may increase as a result of membership. If a country has spare capacity, short-run economic growth may occur as a country enters the EU. This is because consumer spending and investment may increase with the increased confidence that membership brings and net exports may rise. The resulting rise in aggregate demand (AD) will increase real GDP as shown in Figure 2.1.

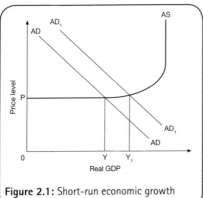

Figure 2.1: Short-run economic growth

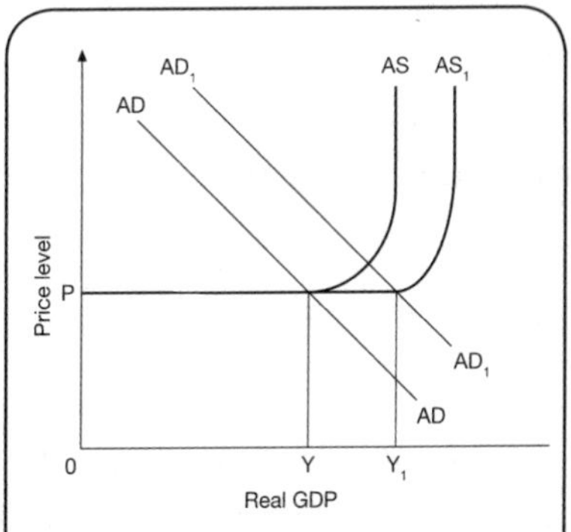

Figure 2.2: Long-run economic growth

Long-run economic growth will occur if the productive potential of the economy increases. Membership may attract increased **foreign direct investment** (FDI) and increase productivity. In this case, the aggregate supply (AS) will move to the right, enabling the economy to experience sustained, non-inflationary growth as illustrated in Figure 2.2. Inflationary pressure may also be kept down by the increased competition that an economy may experience within the EU.

Preparing for membership

Adjustment to being a member of the EU starts some years before full membership. Restrictions on trade, including tariffs and quotas, with EU members are removed and the EU's tariffs on non-member countries are adopted over a period of years. This re-orientates the country's trade towards the EU.

As well as adopting free trade with EU members, candidate countries usually remove any restrictions on capital flows some years before membership. This, and the anticipation of future membership, tends to attract more FDI.

It also takes time to meet the Copenhagen criteria. Former planned economies will probably have to reduce state intervention, build up financial markets and restructure some industries. Some may follow the Russian 'electric shock' means of introducing market reforms, while others may follow a more gradual, step-by-step approach. All economies will have to spend time, money and effort on adopting the laws, rules and policies of the EU. This may, for instance, involve increasing workers' rights and raising environmental standards.

In addition, the EU may make specific recommendations. In 2003, for example, the EU urged some of the countries waiting to join the next year to increase employment in services, reduce reliance on agriculture, raise employment rates, and increase skill levels and flexibility.

The EU does provide a range of advice and financial support to aspiring members to smooth their entry and speed up their convergence and integration.

Experience of former entrants

Entrants into the EU have had mixed experience. Finland responded to the competitive challenge of the EU by increasing its rate of innovation, reforming its industrial structure, and imposing strict monetary and fiscal discipline. Its reward was to be named, in 2004, as the world's most competitive economy.

Ireland is another EU success story, growing rapidly since joining. It has made good use of the EU's structural funds, reduced its budget deficit, invested heavily in education (resulting in a skilled labour force) and has attracted FDI by operating low corporate taxes.

In contrast, Portugal has performed less well to date. Its GDP per head is the lowest of the EU15 and its growth rate has been relatively low.

Initial stages of membership

New members coming into the EU now do not immediately have full access to CAP and structural funding. Limits are placed on the amount they can receive. The NMS began receiving CAP subsidies at 25 per cent of the rate paid to other members. They will not be brought up to full parity with the EU15 until 2013. New members did, however, benefit from a special rural development package in their first two years of membership.

Taking into account the future entry of poorer countries, and the impact that might have on EU expenditure, the European Council in Berlin (1999) placed a cap on the total receipts that any member state may receive from the EU at 4 per cent of the country's GDP.

There can also be a transition period imposed before workers are at full liberty to work anywhere in the EU. New members are now required to be committed to joining the euro. Indeed membership of the euro has been added to the *acquis communautaire*.

The entry of the NMS

1 May 2004 saw the entry of the ten NMS countries. These countries are, on average, significantly poorer than the EU15. Although most of their workers are employed in services, the NMS8 also have much larger agricultural sectors than the EU15 (see Figure 2.3) and a number have relatively high levels of government intervention. Their entry is currently providing both the NMS countries and the EU15 with a range of opportunities and challenges.

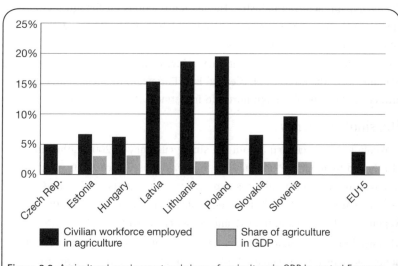

Figure 2.3: Agricultural employment and share of agriculture in GDP in central European New Member States (NMS)

Source: European Commission (data for 2002)

The effect of entry on the NMS

Although it is relatively early to judge, the first years of membership appear to have had a generally favourable impact on the economies of the NMS.

Their experience can be examined by considering a number of different aspects.

Trade

In the build up to entry, the NMS started to trade more with the EU15 and there was a doubling of trade between the two over the period 1995 to 2004. This increased intra-trade has continued.

There was some **trade diversion**. For example, Slovenia had to drop free trade agreements with Serbia, Croatia and Bosnia and the cost of some products rose in Slovenia. However, as the NMS traded mostly with the EU15, **trade creation** effects have proved to be more significant. (See Chapter 7 on trade creation and trade diversion, and EU intra-trade.)

Foreign direct and portfolio investment

Both in the run-up to and since entry, the NMS have been attracting more FDI. Car industry investment, in particular, has been a success across most of the NMS8. Volkswagen is the top exporter from Slovakia, the Czech Republic and Hungary, and Fiat and Daewoo are the biggest foreign investors in Poland's manufacturing industry. The main attractions for foreign investors are relatively low wages, a relatively skilled labour force, flexible labour laws, and low corporate and income taxes.

Portfolio investment has also been increasing. Poland, Hungary and the Czech Republic have the largest CEE (Central East European) financial markets, attracting the bulk of foreign portfolio investment going to the NMS.

The single currency

Slovenia has been cleared to join **the single currency** in 2007. Lithuania had also hoped to adopt the euro in 2007, but was refused because its inflation rate was too high. Currently it is expected to join in 2008 along with Cyprus, Estonia, Latvia and Malta. It is thought Slovakia will join in 2009, the Czech Republic in 2010, Poland in 2011 and Hungary in 2012.

Membership of the single currency has the potential to bring a number of advantages, including increased influence in the EU, more FDI, reduced transactions costs and more discipline on macroeconomic policy. It will, however, reduce macroeconomic sovereignty, with NMS losing national control of their interest rate and exchange rate.

The interest and exchange rate in the eurozone are a 'one size fits all'. If, for example, the NMS were experiencing rapid economic growth, while the rest of the eurozone was experiencing a recession, a decision by the European Central Bank may result in overheating in the NMS. The greater the NMS convergence with the eurozone, the more appropriate the interest rate and the exchange rate will be. (See Chapter 3 for more in depth discussion of the single currency.)

Agriculture

The NMS can now sell their agricultural products to the EU15 without tariffs. They enjoy higher and more stable prices for their produce, which makes planning easier, and can benefit from schemes designed to help them modernise and restructure.

Despite lower wages and lower land rents, however, some NMS farmers face a number of competitive disadvantages relative to EU15 farmers. In general they use less capital, have undeveloped supply chains and as a result are less efficient. It may take some time for their farmers to cut their unit costs.

There are, though, some areas where they actually have a comparative advantage. For example, Poland is strong in processed and frozen fruit and vegetables, which involve a lot of labour in terms of growing and packaging, stressing Poland's low labour cost advantage.

Regions

Many of the regions of the NMS receive EU regional aid, as their incomes per head are low. Large areas of Poland and Latvia, for example, have incomes less than one-third of the EU average. There are indeed only two regions in the NMS8 with incomes above the average. These are Prague, capital of the Czech Republic, and Bratislava, capital of Slovakia.

The effect that EU regional aid will have on the NMS will be influenced significantly by how it is used. Spain, for instance, used a large part of its regional assistance to improve its transport structure. This helped to improve its macroeconomic performance. In contrast, Portugal did not make such good use of the aid it received.

General macroeconomic performance

Table 2.1 shows that the economic growth rate of the NMS has remained high and is forecast to remain so. Their unemployment rates are falling and converging towards those of the EU15. Their budget deficits are also falling and more NMS are moving towards a position where they would meet the requirements to enter the single currency and the Stability and Growth Pact. At the same time, their inflation rates are somewhat higher than those of the EU15.

Of course, there are variations in the macroeconomic performance of the NMS. The Baltic states, in particular, have experienced high growth rates, a relatively rapid fall in unemployment and healthy public finances. They have, however, had problems keeping inflation low. In contrast the Czech Republic and Hungary have had less trouble with inflation, but have also experienced slightly lower economic growth.

The NMS8 have had relatively large current account deficits. These are not considered to be very serious, as they are largely cyclical and not structural, reflecting the more rapid growth of the NMS8 than of the EU15.

Table 2.1: Macroeconomic performance in the EU 2003–2012

Percentage GDP growth						
	2003	2004	2005	2006	2007	2008–2012*
EU15	1.1	2.1	1.5	2.0	2.2	2.2
Eurozone	0.7	1.8	1.4	1.9	2.0	2.1
NMS	4.1	5.1	4.0	4.1	4.1	4.7
EU25	1.2	2.2	1.6	2.1	1.6	2.1

*estimate

Percentage inflation as measured by HICP (harmonised index of consumer prices)						
	2003	2004	2005	2006	2007	2008–2012*
EU15	2.0	2.0	2.2	2.1	2.0	1.9
Eurozone	2.1	2.1	2.2	2.1	2.0	1.8
NMS	1.9	4.2	2.5	2.8	3.0	2.9
EU25	2.0	2.2	2.2	2.1	2.1	2.0

*estimate

Fiscal balance (percentage of GDP)						
	2003	2004	2005	2006	2007	2008–2012*
EU15	-2.8	-2.5	-2.6	-2.5	-2.4	-1.8
Eurozone	-3.0	-2.7	-2.8	-2.7	-2.6	-2.0
NMS	-5.3	-3.8	-3.2	-3.2	-3.2	-2.7
EU25	-3.0	-2.6	-2.6	-2.5	-2.4	-1.9

*estimate

Percentage standardised unemployment rates						
	2003	2004	2005	2006	2007	2008–2012*
EU15	7.9	8.0	7.7	7.7	7.7	7.3
Eurozone	8.7	8.8	8.5	8.4	8.3	7.9
NMS	14.5	14.1	13.3	12.4	12.3	10.7
EU25	8.9	8.9	8.6	8.5	8.4	7.9

*estimate

Source: Table 9 Prospects for the European Union,
National Institute Economic Review No. 195, January 2006

The effect of the entry of the NMS on the EU15

The entry of the NMS has had a number of effects on the EU15.

Administration

The entry of the NMS has made coordination rather more difficult. For example, the number of official languages has risen by 82 per cent to 20. It has not, however, made the EU unmanageable as some feared. It has also given greater impetus to long-overdue reforms to the CAP, regional funding and other EU policies and institutions.

Migration

Migration has increased within the EU. Before entry, twelve of the EU placed temporary restrictions on people from the NMS seeking work in their countries. These restrictions were imposed for fear of the impact of immigration on employment of domestic workers, and the stress more people could place on health care, education and housing services. Similar worries were expressed when Spain and Portugal joined the EU. Immigration from the Iberian economies was actually lower than anticipated and within a short time it was reversed. The increased prosperity at home, brought about in large part by EU membership, actually led to people returning home.

Ireland, Sweden and the UK did not impose restrictions on workers from the NMS, although they have limited access to state benefits. These countries are in need of workers to fill gaps in their labour markets. The UK, in particular, is short of both high- and low-skilled workers including doctors, nurses, teachers, bus drivers, builders, plumbers, waiters and fruit pickers. Employment restrictions on workers from the NMS were removed on 1 May 2006 by a further four member states: Greece, Finland, Portugal and Spain.

Efficiency

The entry of the NMS has increased competition within EU markets. This is putting pressure on EU15 firms to become more efficient. If they respond by increasing their productive and allocative efficiency, the EU will be in a stronger position to face up to the challenge presented by the improving economic performance of the BRICs (Brazil, Russia, India and China) and the USA.

Tax competition

The NMS8 have increased tax competition in the EU. **Flat taxes**, pioneered in Estonia and developed in Slovakia, are now being discussed across the EU.

Markets

The EU15 have been provided with new markets. As incomes are rising in the NMS, EU15 businesses have the potential to increase their sales. The NMS8 are also opening doors to other markets further east and south.

Power

The enlargement has made the EU a more powerful economic bloc and has increased its relative bargaining strength at the IMF (International Monetary Fund), WTO, and in direct negotiations with the USA and NAFTA. The EU has a larger population than the USA, but not yet a higher GDP.

Bulgaria, Romania and Croatia

Bulgaria and Romania signed an EU accession treaty on 25 April 2005 and will join the EU on 1 January 2007 if it is considered that they have implemented sufficient market reforms, reduced corruption and crime, improved environmental controls and met the other requirements of the Copenhagen criteria.

In the period 2004 to 2006 their economic performance improved, with economic growth rising and unemployment and inflation falling. Concerns, however, have been expressed about the high proportion (45 per cent) of the Romanian labour force employed in agriculture and the low productivity of that agriculture. Their GDP per head is only just over 30 per cent of the EU average and Romania will be the poorest country to join the EU.

After Bulgaria and Romania, Croatia is set to be the next member. It implemented a Stabilisation and Association Agreement in February 2005. Croatia has a higher GDP per head than Bulgaria and Romania, a rapid rate of economic growth, is attracting a high level of FDI and is experiencing a property boom. It does, however, have problems with structural unemployment and still needs to improve the efficiency of its public administration.

Turkey

Turkey applied to join the EU more than 40 years ago and has seen a number of countries join while it has been waiting. In 1996 an EU–Turkey customs union was formed and the country became an official EU candidate country in 1999. EU membership talks were formally launched in October 2005, but these accession negotiations are expected to last at least ten years. Turkey has carried out a number of human rights reforms including abolishing the death penalty, improving women's rights and showing greater respect for Kurdish culture. It has also improved its economic performance, significantly reducing inflation (see Figure 2.4).

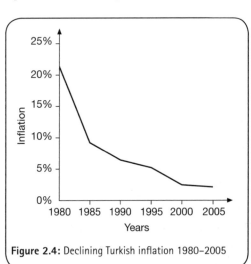

Figure 2.4: Declining Turkish inflation 1980–2005

Those in the EU – particularly in Austria, France and the Netherlands – who oppose Turkish membership point to the risk of large-scale immigration from Turkey, the impact on the EU budget and the differences between Turkey and EU countries. These differences include the following.

- It is larger than most countries in the EU. It has a population of 71 million. If it joins the EU, it will overtake Germany as the biggest member within fifteen years and will have the most individual votes in Brussels.
- It is poor. Turkey's GDP per head is only 29 per cent of the EU average. A third of its population work on the land, and it is one of the largest debtors to the IMF. Turkey's poverty and large agricultural sectors could mean relatively big budgetary transfers from the EU budget for many years.
- Not all of it is in Europe. However, the EU conceded as far back as 1963 that Turkey was sufficiently European to be a candidate one day.

- It is Muslim, although the Turkish government is secular. Currently 12 million EU citizens are Muslims and the EU's founding articles include respect for religious freedom.

There are potential benefits to the EU from Turkey joining including:
- its young and growing population could fill skill gaps in EU15 countries which have ageing populations
- it could rebalance the EU – at the moment it is somewhat skewed towards small countries
- it will increase the economic bargaining power of the EU.

Future further enlargement

A queue of other countries are waiting to join the EU including Albania, Bosnia, Macedonia, Montenegro and Serbia. This indicates that there is a belief that a larger EU can still bring benefits to new members. Whether further enlargement will bring benefits to both new and established members will be influenced by whether the new members have similar political institutions and convergent economic performance.

Summary

On completion of this chapter you have learnt:
- that countries wishing to join the EU have to possess a functioning market economy, have a democratic political system, and accept EU laws and regulations
- the entry of new members is more likely to be beneficial if their economies are converging with established members and if they integrate relatively quickly
- countries joining the EU hope to experience greater political stability and higher economic growth
- countries prepare for membership by removing restrictions on the movement of products and capital with the EU and reforming their economic institutions, economic policies and political systems
- in the early years of membership, countries may not receive full access to EU funds, may have restrictions imposed on the movement of their workers to other EU countries and will be expected to prepare for membership of the single currency

- the NMS have lower incomes per GDP and generally larger agricultural sectors
- NMS are now trading more with the EU, are attracting more FDI and improving their macroeconomic performance
- the entry of the NMS has put pressure on the EU to reform some of its policies and on the EU15 to increase their competitiveness
- there is dispute on whether and when Turkey should be allowed to join.

Further reading

Grant, S., Vidler, C., Section 4.4 in *Heinemann Economics A2 for AQA*, Heinemann, 2003

Grant, S., Vidler, C., Section 6.2 in *Heinemann Economics for OCR*, Heinemann, 2003

Jovanovic, M., Chapter 14 in *The Economics of European Integration*, Edward Elgar Pub, 2004

Useful websites

EU enlargement policy:
www.europa.eu.int/comm/dgs/enlargement/index-en.htm

Activities

Topics for investigation

Using eurostat (www.europa.eu.int/comm/eurostat), find information on the economic performance of Greece and Turkey. Analyse whether their economies are converging.

Exam-style practice questions

Data response question
Romania

Romania, the largest Balkan country, is pressing ahead with a number of reforms in preparation for its entry into the EU. It is seeking to reduce corruption at all levels of government and in the judiciary. It is also trying to implement a large number of EU laws and regulations (the *acquis communautaire*), including food hygiene rules and removing tariff barriers.

Romania hopes to reap considerable benefits from all the hard work it is undertaking. It hopes to attract significantly more FDI, sell more to EU countries and to enjoy greater freedom of movement for its people within the EU.

Membership will, however, also bring fresh challenges. Romanian firms will have to face more competition from its EU partners. If they respond to this increased competition by raising their efficiency, Romania's citizens should enjoy higher incomes in the future, and the gap between the country's GDP per capita and those of other former planned economies, such as Hungary and Poland, should narrow.

Table A: Selected economic figures for Hungary, Poland and Romania in 2003

	Population (m)	GDP per capita ($)	GDP annual growth (%)	FDI per capita net inflow ($)
Hungary	10.0	14 574	2.9	2 089
Poland	38.3	10 854	3.7	1 105
Romania	21.7	6 974	4.9	486

1. What conditions do countries have to meet to join the EU? (3)

2. Describe the differences between the Hungarian, Polish and Romanian economies shown in Table A. (6)

3. a) Explain why membership of the EU may result in an economy attracting more FDI. (6)

   b) Discuss the benefits an economy can gain from increased FDI. (10)

Essay questions

1. a) Explain what is meant by long-run economic growth. (10)

   b) Discuss the costs and benefits of economic growth. (15)

2. a) Explain why convergence is important for the successful operation of EU policies. (10)

   b) Discuss the extent to which membership of the EU is beneficial for a country's economy. (15)

3 The EU and national governments

In this chapter you will learn:

- how the EU, through various policies, interacts with the activities of member states
- how the EU's budget is funded and how it is used
- what is meant by Economic and Monetary Union, its benefits and costs, particularly from a UK standpoint
- why the EU needs a comprehensive, integrated transport policy
- how the EU tackles its regional problem
- why there is a growing need for an effective environmental policy
- why some of the EU's policies have taken on an added significance in the EU25.

> **Key words** additionality • cohesion • competitiveness
> Common Transport Policy • convergence criteria
> Economic and Monetary Union • European Central Bank
> exchange rate uncertainty • external economies of scale
> fiscal policy • Growth and Stability Pact • harmonisation
> liberalisation • mutual recognition • 'polluter pays' principle
> price transparency • regional problem • social dumping
> transaction costs

The EU budget

In some respects, the EU's budget is like that of each of its 25 member states – each year money raised from taxpayers and from governmental contributions is used to fund the various EU policies and programmes for the benefit of its citizens. Unlike domestic budgets though, the size of the EU budget is relatively small. In 2006, for example, it was just over 1 per cent of the combined gross national income of the member states.

Despite its small size, historically, the EU budget has been controversial from a political standpoint. The UK has fought long and hard to retain its annual rebate, while of late, Poland especially of the NMS8 countries, has been critical of the resources that have been allocated to the poorer new member states, itself included.

The EU's income comes from three sources:

- customs duties, accruing from those imports that are subject to a common external tariff
- a share of the harmonised VAT receipts of member states
- a contribution from member states, based on the size of their gross national income.

The EU's expenditure can be broken down into five main headings (see Figure 3.1 below).

- **Competitiveness** and **cohesion** (39 per cent). This is the largest item and consists of money that is available to make the EU more competitive (research, energy and transport expenditure, for example). To aid cohesion, payments are made to less prosperous regions and social programmes, for example. The need for this latter type of spending has increased with the 2004 enlargement.
- Managing natural resources. This includes agriculture, which in 2006 took up around 36 per cent of total expenditure. The remaining expenditure in this heading was for rural development programmes and environmental policies.
- Citizenship, freedom, security and justice. Although very small in budgetary terms, this item covers the EU's protection of its borders from illegal immigrants, the fight against terrorism, and control against diseases such as rabies and bird flu. Its purpose is to foster cooperation between member states in tackling issues of wider importance for the well-being of all concerned.

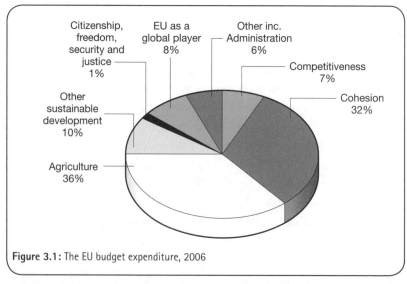

Figure 3.1: The EU budget expenditure, 2006

- EU as a global player. This type of expenditure has taken on a new significance over the past few years. It includes help in preparing CEE countries for accession, the reconstruction of the Balkans and Iraq, compensation for sugar-producing African, Caribbean and Pacific (ACP) countries, aid for the Asian tsunami and similar EU-wide initiatives.
- Administrative costs. This is self-explanatory and covers the cost of the Commission, the European Parliament and related activities.

Common Agricultural Policy expenditure

As Figure 3.1 indicates, the funding of the CAP remains the largest single item in the 2006 budget. In relative terms, the percentage of the budget spent on agriculture has fallen over the last 30 years. It was over 70 per cent in 1973 when the UK joined the EU, and many people feel that it is still too high (see Chapter 6). In 2005, the Commission proposed that budget expenditure should be restructured, so that an increasing percentage could be allocated to competitiveness.

Unless there is a major breakthrough by the WTO in persuading the EU to cut back its farm subsides, the proportion of the budget spent on agriculture will not fall. A reallocation of funds will be needed in 2007/08 with the likely accession of Romania and Bulgaria, which have large agricultural sectors.

Income and distribution

Referring back to the sources of the EU's budgetary income, most comes from member states, depending on the size of their national incomes. So, richer countries pay rather more into the budget than relatively poorer countries, such as Portugal, Greece and the 2004 NMS.

However, the distribution of funds is not related to the size of a country's economy. Distribution is actually based on the extent to which member states qualify for expenditure through specific EU policies. So, member states with large agricultural sectors and a number of poor regions benefit more than those with very few farmers and no particular regional problem.

UK objections

In the case of the UK, in 1984, Mrs Thatcher maintained that the net contribution made to the budget was unacceptable. As a consequence, a special rebate was agreed, in part for fear that the UK might withdraw completely from the EU. Other net contributors such as Austria, Germany, the Netherlands and Sweden resent this special treatment. In a similar way, poorer member states argue that the rebate paid to the UK could be used in a more positive way, for example, through more resources being allocated to EU policies designed to enhance the degree of cohesion across all member states.

The latest budgetary crisis was at the end of 2005, when the UK agreed to a cut in the rebate that had been agreed 20 years previously (see box below). It remains to be seen whether this significant political gesture will lead to more substantial reform of a budget that is still very heavily weighted in favour of France's inefficient agricultural producers.

EU leaders agree new budget plan

European leaders have agreed the next seven-year EU budget after two days of tense talks. The budget figure agreed for 2007–13 was 1.045 per cent of gross national income, well below the 1.24 per cent sought by the Commission. The UK has given up almost 20 per cent of its rebate (£7 billion) in order to help fund the economic development of new member states. In return, France has agreed to a budget review in 2008/09 that could lead to a cut in farm subsidies. The deal was warmly greeted by the Polish delegation who had been concerned that the EU was not being fair to the new member states, who wanted a larger share of the funding for less prosperous member states.

This deal has come about because six member states, including the biggest contributors – the UK, France, Germany, the Netherlands, Austria and Sweden – wanted the budget to be limited to 1 per cent gross national income. The additional resources will be spent on three main areas: sustainable development, citizenship and strengthening the EU as a global player.

Source: BBC News, 17 December 2005 (adaptation)

Economic and monetary union

The development of the EMU

On 1 January 2002, the euro, the new European single currency, became the 'real' currency for those living in twelve of the EU15 member states. Three years prior to this, the euro had become the technical official currency of eleven members, when they agreed to irrevocably fix their exchange rates against the euro. (Greece joined a little later.) The UK had declined the offer to join, while Sweden and Denmark rejected the euro through referenda. The launch of the euro represented the largest currency conversion that has ever been attempted, and at the time was seen as moving the EU much closer to political union.

There is much more to **Economic and Monetary Union** (EMU) than the single currency, although the euro is its most obvious sign. As the name suggests, EMU involves the next stage in the integration of the economic policies and the monetary sectors of its participants. More specifically, it involves:

- economic union; this has been largely achieved through the Single European Act of 1986, which set about dismantling the remaining non-tariff barriers to trade and to the free movement of factors of production; it also involved greater harmonisation of policies – for example, tax harmonisation
- monetary union; namely, fixing exchange rates once and for all, removing any remaining barriers to capital flows and establishing a common interest rate, to be determined independently by the European Central Bank (ECB).

By definition, participation in the EMU requires national governments to hand over considerable sovereignty in their ability to manage their own economic affairs. This crucial requirement has been central and fundamental to the UK's non-participation.

The progress of EMU

EMU has been on the European agenda for many years. It was first suggested as the way forward for the EU in 1969. However, the birth of EMU as it now exists dates back to the so-called Delors' Report of 1988, in which the then-President of the European Commission proposed a three-stage process to EMU. Negotiations were finally completed with the signing of the Maastricht Treaty in 1993. This paved the way for the euro by setting out five **convergence criteria** that prospective members had to meet before being eligible to sign up for EMU.

1. Inflation rates at no more than 1.5 percentage points above the average of the three countries with the lowest inflation rates.
2. Long-term interest rates at no more than 2 percentage points above the average of the three countries with the lowest interest rates.
3. A stable exchange rate within ERM for the previous two years.
4. Budget deficits of less than 3 per cent of GDP.
5. National debt of less than 60 per cent of GDP or falling towards this level.

In May 1998, towards the end of stage two on the road to EMU, the European Council agreed that, with a little last-minute data manipulation, twelve member states had met the convergence criteria. These included Denmark which had decided not to join, but not Greece, which was struggling to satisfy four of the five criteria. The door was left open for Greece to join some time after the beginning of 1999.

The Stability and Growth Pact

It was also necessary to underpin the euro with a strict fiscal discipline. Germany, especially, had been concerned that some of the weaker countries might use large budget deficits to manage their economies once the single currency came into being. So, in June 1997, the European Council agreed the **Stability and Growth Pact** that prohibited members of EMU from having a budget deficit above 3 per cent of GDP. This was a further diminution of the economic sovereignty and power of member states to manage their own economic affairs.

Benefits of economic and monetary union

In theory there are four main benefits that arise from participation in EMU.

Reduced exchange rate uncertainty

Permanent conversion rates between the euro and the external exchange rates of the currencies of participants were finalised by the EU's finance ministers on 31 December 1998. This brought to an end any uncertainty arising from exchange rate variations that had previously occurred, even within the confines of the ERM. The main benefit is trade: the prices exporters receive and the prices paid by importers are known at the time of the trade contract. They are not affected by exchange rate fluctuations. This removes the need for 'hedging', where goods are sold for an agreed price at some future date. Economists have long argued that reducing **exchange rate uncertainty** allows countries to fully exploit their comparative advantage (see Chapter 7). However, where exchange rates fluctuate (often quite widely), countries are reluctant to reallocate resources to benefit from this comparative advantage. It is also argued that when economic conditions are more stable, businesses will restructure production in order to benefit from economies of scale (see Chapter 4). Over the longer term, it is believed that all of this will accelerate the pace of economic integration.

Price transparency

A single currency allows consumers and businesses to compare relative prices across all countries that have signed up for the euro. This transparency should make markets more competitive, because if prices in a market are uncompetitive, there is pressure for them to be reduced. This may not happen in practice, largely because of the differences in indirect taxes and living standards between member states.

Table 3.1 shows some examples of price variations of selected branded goods between member states. This can be rather confusing. For instance, it is unrealistic to suggest that Greek people should travel all the way to Italy to buy ice cream because it is much cheaper there! What is much more likely is that businesses will be more inclined to source from low cost providers, once transport costs have been taken into account.

Table 3.1: Examples of highest and lowest average supermarket prices in EU12 countries in 2004

Branded products	Lowest	Highest
Häagen-Dazs ice cream	Italy (60)	Greece (117)
Barilla Pasta	Italy (55)	Ireland (114)
Red Bull	Austria (79)	Finland (134)
Own label products		
Canned pineapple	Netherlands (53)	Finland (181)
Rice	Portugal (45)	Sweden (182)
Hairspray	Sweden (47)	Ireland (142)

(EU12 average = 100)

Transactions costs

This is the term that is used for the cost of changing from one currency into another. With a single currency these costs no longer apply. For EU member states outside EMU, **transactions costs** remain and have to be paid. These transaction costs can amount to a few per cent of the total cost of any personal or business transaction.

Low interest rates, low inflation

Advocates of EMU believe that the **European Central Bank's** (ECB's) aim is to keep inflation among its members at a low level and that, in turn, allows a low rate of interest to be set for the eurozone. For countries like Greece and Spain that have traditionally experienced high inflation, this aspect of EMU provides welcome relief from having to battle domestically against high inflation. Greece and Spain would previously have tackled high inflation with high interest rates, but they cannot do this under the EMU. They have to adopt the low EU interest rate. It is interesting to note that the ECB's interest rate has been below that of UK's Bank of England for some time.

Costs of economic and monetary union

Loss of monetary sovereignty

The most controversial aspect of EMU is popularly referred to as the 'one size fits all' issue. This refers to the fact that once a member state signs up to join the euro, monetary sovereignty is lost to the ECB. As a result, members are required to accept the ECB's interest rate – they cannot set their own interest rate in line with their own prevailing economic conditions. This aspect of economic policy has been a very important cause for concern in the UK and has been a major consideration in the UK's 'wait and see' attitude to EMU.

This problem can be seen in a simplified way in Table 3.2. A single interest rate is most effective when the economies of all members of the eurozone are similar in terms of inflation and unemployment rates. Table 3.2 shows how these varied in 2003.

The arrows show the direction of change since 2002, when the euro came into being as an internationally traded currency. In its first few months, the euro depreciated against the pound and the US dollar. At the same time, six member states experienced rising unemployment and falling inflation. Ireland was one of these, but still had the second lowest unemployment rate and second highest inflation rate of the eleven members shown in the table. Unemployment in three other members was either rising or stable, but in all cases it was substantially higher than in Ireland.

It could be assumed from Table 3.2 that the ECB's rate of interest might be lowered to reduce unemployment or, at worst, remain low to stimulate monetary demand. This is not necessarily the best policy for Ireland, as it could trigger a further inflationary boom, in addition to that it had already experienced in the build up to the euro's launch. The high level of unemployment in France and Germany, the eurozone's largest economies, is cause for concern and will certainly override any attempt to raise the ECB's interest rate.

Table 3.2: Eurozone unemployment and inflation rates in 2003

Eurozone member[1]	Unemployment (per cent)[2]	Inflation (per cent change in consumer prices)[2]
Austria	4.35 ↑	1.36 ↓
Belgium	8.30 ↑	1.50 ↓
Finland	9.00 –	0.90 ↓
France	9.54 ↑	2.11 ↑
Germany	10.50 ↑	1.07 ↓
Greece	7.90 ↓	3.60 –
Ireland	4.70 ↑	3.50 ↓
Italy	8.98 ↓	2.46 ↓
Netherlands	5.50 ↑	2.10 ↓
Portugal	6.50 ↑	3.30 ↓
Spain	11.30 –	3.00 ↓

Note: [1] excludes Luxembourg
[2] the direction of the arrows shows the change from 2002
Note: Equivalent UK figures were: unemployment 5.1 per cent, inflation 1.36 per cent

Source: Economist Intelligence Unit

The loss of monetary sovereignty clearly poses problems for those member states whose economy is out of line with the eurozone norm. Referring back to Table 3.2, this would include Ireland, Austria and the Netherlands, all of which have unemployment rates way below the average. If unemployment in these countries was falling, rather than rising, they could face inflationary pressure if, as seems likely, interest rates remain at a low level.

The answer to such a difficulty is that **fiscal policy** can still be used by eurozone members to stabilise their economies. During a relative boom period, aggregate demand can be cut through tax increases or reductions in government spending. At a time of recession, aggregate demand can be increased through reverse fiscal measures. This is a very simplified view and might require some qualification in view of the relationship between government borrowing and interest rates; increased borrowing tends to raise interest rates.

Reduction in fiscal sovereignty

In 1997, in order to control the use of fiscal measures, the Stability and Growth Pact was agreed by EU leaders (see also earlier). This restriction was designed to keep ECB interest rates at a low level. Without it, interest rates could rise if governments borrowed excessively to finance their deficits. Any country that does not meet the pact's requirements could be fined by the European Commission. That was the position at the pact's launch. By 2003, these seemingly iron rules were turned into more of a 'gentleman's agreement' following serious problems in the French and German economies (see box below). Unlike most other examples in this chapter, this is more a case of two national governments using their political power to combat an EU policy very much to their own benefit.

The pact that was

1997	*EU leaders agree details of Growth and Stability Pact*
January 2002	*Launch of euro notes and coins*
February 2002	*Members refuse to endorse formal 'early warning' to Germany over raising budget deficit*
June 2002	*Members renege on earlier agreement to run balanced budgets by 2004*
October 2002	*France refuses to cut its deficit budget as the state of its economy deteriorates further*
October 2003	*France and Germany advise other members that they will break the deficit budget rules for the third successive year*
November 2003	*Sanctions mechanism against France and Germany suspended, much to the annoyance of some of the smaller members*

Consumer cost

A final, and in some respects short-term, cost of EMU is that is has been seen by most consumers as inflationary (see following box). Three years after the launch of the euro, an EU survey in March 2005 showed that over 90 per cent of people in the eurozone believed that the introduction of the euro had sent prices soaring. In France, Greece and Spain, the figure was higher at 98 per cent.

EU officials blamed small businesses for taking advantage of the switch to euros. They argued that inflation had been held steady at around 2 per cent in the eurozone, despite the rising price of oil and the increased taxes on cigarettes and alcohol. The fear, along with Italy's threat to dump the euro, was that the sense of gloom was adversely affecting the public's perception of the benefits of a single currency.

Greek shoppers boycott shops

Greek people boycotted shops and markets yesterday in protest at price rises since the euro was introduced at the start of this year. The Greek government had already appealed to retailers to keep prices down, and threatened a 'black-list' for unjustified increases. Price controls are against eurozone free market principles. Prior to using the euro, there were about 340 drachma to one new euro. The rounding up of prices by opportunist retailers led to a 15 per cent increase in food prices since January. Among the products with high increases are olive oil and fish (12 per cent) and bottled water (over 100 per cent).

Source: *The Times*, 4 September, 2002 (adaptation)

The UK and EMU

The five criteria

In 1997, the Chancellor of the Exchequer, Gordon Brown, backed the euro in principle, but made it clear that the time was not right for the UK to join the first wave of participants in 1999. He published five criteria (the so-called Five Tests) for joining EMU. These were:

- whether there can be sustainable convergence between the UK and the other economies of a single currency
- whether there is sufficient flexibility to cope with economic change
- the effect on investment
- the impact on the financial services industry
- whether it is good for employment.

Since then, the UK has played a waiting game. At one stage, 2001 was suggested as the possible date for a referendum on the issue. Later the Chancellor made it clear that there would be a decision in June 2003 when a report on whether the five tests had been met was produced. It was concluded that four had not been met. The one exception was that entry would benefit the country's financial services industry. More recently, a referendum seems ever further in the future.

Sustainable convergence

Of the tests, the first is most important. The UK economy is not aligned to the eurozone. The pattern of trade is different (see Chapter 7), labour and product markets are more flexible and the UK economy is much more sensitive to interest rate changes. Although UK interest rates are higher, unemployment in recent years has been well below that of the eurozone, while economic growth has outstripped that in the eurozone by a considerable amount. In short, the UK has not faced the severe recessionary forces that have caused problems for France and Germany.

The effect on investment is also controversial. As shown in Chapter 7, the UK has attracted more FDI than any other EU member. Opinion is divided as to whether this will be at risk if the UK remains outside the eurozone. However, FDI has tailed off in recent years, with some multinational corporations (MNCs) openly stating that they will not increase their investment until it is known that the UK will join the euro. 'When rather than if' remains the likely scenario... but just when remains highly problematic.

The great EMU debate – is the UK better 'in' or 'out'?

For

- Inward investment is at risk if the UK stays out – jobs will be diverted to eurozone members.
- Interest rates are likely to be permanently low.
- The euro exchange rate will be more stable than the pound on international currency markets. This provides protection against speculation.
- Outside EMU, the UK will be peripheral to decision-making and left behind.

Against

- The UK has had the strongest economy in the eurozone in recent years.
- A single currency is irreversible – there would be no going back to the pound.
- Economic conditions will never be the same across the whole of the eurozone.
- Weaker countries, maybe the UK, will experience higher unemployment.
- Centralisation and loss of sovereignty will deepen.
- Joining EMU implies a commitment to greater political integration.

Transport policy

Article 3 of the Treaty of Rome stated that the EU should establish 'a common policy in the sphere of transport'. This was seen as essential to enable the free movement of goods and people across the national boundaries of member states. In other words, it was necessary to ensure that the full benefits of the customs union were being realised. Given the geographical location of the Six, subsequent articles in the Treaty of Rome elaborated the principles as they should apply to road and rail transport. Other modes of transport were not explicitly referred to.

Unlike the CAP, where agreement was reached within a few years of the EU being established, the development of a meaningful **Common Transport Policy** (CTP) has been a slow and painful task. Its development has been consistently held back by the protectionist attitudes of some member states, a problem that appears to have deepened as the EU has expanded. The CTP is a particularly good example of a policy that few would disagree with, yet where national interests have invariably come before the common good.

Table 3.3: The freight transport market in selected EU member states in 2002 (billion tonne kms)

EU members	Road		Rail		Inland waterways	
	Total	%	Total	%	Total	%
Belgium	39.6	72.0	7.3	13.3	8.1	14.7
France	277.2	82.6	50.0	14.9	8.3	2.5
Germany	349.3	71.3	76.3	15.6	64.2	13.1
Greece	20.4	98.6	0.3	1.4	–	–
Ireland	10.7	96.4	0.4	3.6	–	–
Italy	192.7	90.4	20.4	9.6	0.1	–
Netherlands	41.4	48.0	4.0	4.7	40.8	47.3
Spain	161.3	93.3	11.6	6.7	–	–
UK	161.5	89.5	18.7	10.4	0.2	0.1

Source: Transport Statistics, Great Britain, 2005 edition (adaptation)

Diverse freight transport in member states

One reason why agreement on the contents of a CTP has been fraught is the diverse nature of the freight transport market between member states. This is summarised in Table 3.3 which shows, of the principal member states:

- the UK, Italy and Spain have freight markets that are dominated by road transport
- other member states, the Netherlands and Germany, and to a lesser extent France, have market situations where customers have rather more modal choice
- rail freight has a place in all cases, but to a varying degree. Of the member states shown, the UK is the only one where rail freight demand and market share have increased in recent years. (For more details see Bamford C. G., *Transport Economics*, Heinemann, 2006.)

Although data is not shown in Table 3.3, most of the NMS8 member states have strong rail freight sectors in terms of market share, but these are declining at the expense of road freight and distribution.

Infrastructure

For the past 40 years or so, an objective of the CTP has been to develop high quality transport infrastructure to ease the flows of goods within and between member states. European funding has consistently been provided to finance a system of 'E' routes and to upgrade the Trans-European express rail passenger routes. At a regional level, the European Regional Development Fund (ERDF) has supported transport developments in less prosperous regions. For example, the AI(M) upgrade in north-east England and the extension of the autostrade network into the Italian Mezzogiorno are just two examples of many such projects.

Completion of the SEM

The function of transport in the EU is to facilitate the free flow of goods and people. In the year prior to the Maastricht Treaty and the political discussion to complete the Single European Market (SEM), this was by no means the case. The obstacles to the movement of goods were particularly frustrating for businesses involved in intra-EU trade. Also, border checks on passenger transport had not been removed between all member states. There was clearly a need to remove the many non–tariff barriers if transport was to fulfill its function within the SEM. (See Chapter 4 for details of the SEM.)

The need to complete the SEM, therefore, gave a new impetus to the CTP. By the end of 1992, it was intended that three important principles had to be agreed if this were to be achieved.

- **Liberalisation** or deregulation. This involves the removal of unduly restrictive regulations that limit the entry of new firms into transport markets. In road freight transport especially, it was difficult, due to cabotage restrictions, for there to be a competitive market whereby hauliers across member states were able to compete in each other's domestic markets. (Cabotage is the ability of a haulier based in one EU country to carry out work without restriction in the market of another EU country. Up to 1999, this type of movement was restricted by permits given to hauliers to do this type of work.) The air passenger transport market was heavily regulated through restrictive bilateral agreements, usually between national carriers. A liberalised transport market would in principle allow market forces to have a full role to play in the allocation of resources.

- **Harmonisation.** This involves the removal of distortions to competition between transport operators in different member states. It is sometimes referred to as establishing 'a level playing field' particularly in terms of indirect taxation, subsidies and the regulations and directives that apply to transport operators. In a single market, there should be one common system that applies to all.
- **Mutual recognition.** This is a situation whereby a common set of standards are applied and accepted by all member states and covers a wide range of issues such as customs checks, the design of vehicles, licences and qualifications.

Two market liberalisations

Despite endless negotiations, not all of the above was in place by 1 January 1993. France and Germany maintained that liberalisation could not be achieved without harmonisation. The UK and some other member states took a different view. They argued that harmonisation would most likely follow once liberalisation had been achieved. It was not until the late 1990s that two important markets were fully liberalised. These were as follows.

- Road freight and logistics. From July 1998, any EU-based road freight and logistics business has been able to move goods anywhere within the EU and has been free to set up in business in any other member state. This has brought new market opportunities for businesses and a wider choice of haulier for customers.
- Air passenger services. These have been fully deregulated since 1997, the outcome of which has been to improve competition between national carriers and, significantly, allow the entry of low-fare carriers into the market. Few would argue that this has not been beneficial from a consumer's standpoint as fares have fallen and new services have started up.

Harmonisation

At the present time, the EU's transport market is liberalised. This applies across the EU25. Far less progress has been made with respect to harmonisation. A major stumbling block has been that from a fiscal policy standpoint, member states retain considerable control over the rates of indirect taxation that are charged on transport. A particularly contentious issue from a UK perspective is the price of fuel, particularly diesel fuel, as this is universally used by vehicles moving goods around the EU. Table 3.4 shows the position in 2004.

Table 3.4: Average price of 100 litres of diesel fuel in selected EU member states in 2004 (US$)

Member state	Average price	% tax
Belgium	109	55
France	110	64
Germany	116	64
Greece	92	48
Ireland	110	59
Italy	117	60
Netherlands	110	57
Spain	94	53
UK	150	72

Source: Transport Statistics, Great Britain, 2005 edition (adaptation)

The UK is very much the 'odd European out'. The average price of diesel fuel is substantially more expensive than elsewhere in the EU. In part, this is due to the high taxation imposed by the UK government. Given the importance of fuel costs for road transport companies, it is easy to see why many UK-based hauliers claim that they are struggling to remain competitive relative to providers in other member states. The UK industry is also most heavily taxed in terms of annual standing charges for operating goods vehicles.

Some harmonisation has been agreed, mainly in terms of the use of tachographs, the regulation of the work done by road goods vehicle drivers, and the maximum weights and dimensions of vehicles.

Trans-European Rail Freight Network (TERFN)

A more positive achievement of the CTP has been the decision taken in late 1999 to establish a Trans-European Rail Freight Network (TERFN), in order to reduce bottlenecks to the movement of goods within Europe as a whole. This is consistent with the EU's long-standing commitment to see a better use made of its rail network. It is also a very clear indication of support for rail over road transport from a sustainability standpoint, by increasing the market share of rail freight. The TERFN system, given time, will consist of specific links and nodes across member states where a high quality international rail freight service is provided. This network is additional to that for high speed rail passenger, conventional rail and combined (road/rail) transport across the EU.

In recent years, more positive progress has been made towards a CTP that will enhance competitiveness and allow for the further economic and political integration of the EU. The accession of the NMS8 member states presents an enormous challenge in view of their heavy reliance on largely outdated rail networks. Notwithstanding this challenge, at a time when economic integration has slowed down, the liberalisation of the EU's transport markets is an important recent success.

Regional policy

The EU has a persistent **regional problem**, the term used to describe a situation whereby living standards vary both within and between member states. Figure 3.2 shows the extent of current variations, measured in terms of purchasing power standards (PPS) for the EU25, plus Romania and Bulgaria. This figure shows two types of variation.

- Differences *within* member states. The largest difference is in the UK, where there is a factor of 4.3 between inner London (315 per cent of EU25 average) and Cornwall and the Isles of Scilly (73 per cent of the EU25 average). Substantial variations can also be found in older member states, such as Belgium and France, and within the Czech Republic, Hungary and Slovakia among the NMS8 countries.
- Differences between member states (see Chapter 5). Luxembourg, for example, has average living standards around four times those of the poorest new member, Latvia. Of the NMS8 countries, only Slovenia has living standards that approach the EU average.

Geographically, for the EU15, the regional problem was largely of a core-periphery nature. Centrally placed parts of the EU such as the Île de France and Randstadt Holland areas were substantially more prosperous than far-flung regions in East Germany, Scotland and the south of Italy. With the most recent enlargement, the peripheral dimension has been stretched eastwards.

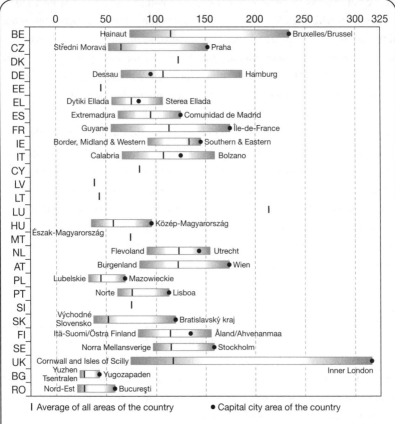

Figure 3.2: GDP per inhabitant (in PPS) 2002, in percentage of EU25 average (EU25 = 100)

Ever since the Treaty of Rome, which stressed the need for the harmonious development of economies 'by reducing the differences existing among various regions', there has been a strongly open commitment to regional policy from within the EU. This commitment has more recently been demonstrated through the Single European Act, and provisions for the accession of CEE members. This area of economic policy is also one where national governments of member states have taken a keen interest *from time to time.*

Intervention

There is a need for intervention because the market system does not function effectively when dealing with regional problems. Figure 3.3 shows a highly simplified version of what should happen if there are regional disparities. Labour can be expected to migrate to where there are job opportunities and, in turn, capital is expected to flow into less prosperous regions where labour

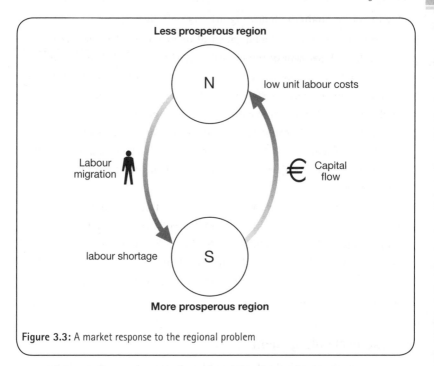

Figure 3.3: A market response to the regional problem

is available at low cost. Low wage regions can expect to be made more prosperous through this response. The reality is that the market does not behave like this; it fails to allocate resources in an efficient way because labour is invariably unwilling to migrate and business capital is often also immobile, firms preferring to remain where they can benefit from **external economies of scale**. In such circumstances, a regional policy, EU-led or from national governments, is needed to redress the situation in less prosperous regions.

Structural funding

The focus of EU regional policy until 2000 was through 'structural' funding mechanisms, the main ones being as follows.

- European Regional Development Fund (ERDF). This provides support for the development of infrastructure in less prosperous regions.
- European Social Fund (ESF). Support is provided for people living in designated areas where local employment has been adversely affected.
- European Agricultural Guidance and Guarantee Fund (EAGGF), which provides price guarantees and funds for a range of agricultural projects.
- Financial Instrument for Fisheries Guidance (FIGG).

In addition, there was a cohesion fund that provided financial support for a range of projects. More recently, these structural funds have been required to enable the EU to attain the following priority objectives.

1. To promote the structural adjustment of regions where GDP per head is less than 75 per cent of the EU average. These are called Objective 1 regions and cover large parts of Spain, Greece, eastern Germany, western Ireland, southern Italy, most of Wales, Cornwall and the Yorkshire coalfield. (Using all the above funds, as listed above.)

2. To support the economic and social conversion of regions facing structural difficulties, for example, a loss of manufacturing and extractive employment. These Objective 2 regions have benefited from ERDF and ESF funding.

3. To support the adaptation and modernisation of policies and systems of education, training and employment. Here the ESF has managed labour market polices designed to enhance the access of Objective 3-based workers back into the labour force. (Objective 3 workers include unemployed graduates, married women returning to the workforce and those seeking a skills upgrade.)

Geographical enlargement

The May 2004 geographical enlargement has presented a major challenge to the EU's regional policy. For a start, financial resources available through structural funding mechanisms will be subject to increased competition, with some resources inevitably being reallocated from the EU15 to the new accessionaries. This will not be popular in those parts of the EU that have received substantial benefit from these funding mechanisms in the past. Funding the promises made to the new member states will put a strain on the EU's budget, adding to the pressures to ensure that future funding is spent only on projects where there is every opportunity of reducing regional disparities.

Over the last ten years or so, the structural and cohesion funds have had a decisive role in increasing investment in physical as well as human capital in those regions where they apply. The result of their strengthening has been that GDP per head in the poorest regions has grown at around 3 per cent per annum, compared with 2 per cent for the rest of the EU. This has to been seen as a very positive outcome.

Environmental policy

Unlike some other policies discussed in this chapter, the Treaty of Rome had no provision for a common environmental policy. However, this is an area of policy where the national governments of member states have been actively engaged since the 1960s. It is also an area of increasing importance as far as an EU policy is concerned. Members believe that high environmental standards stimulate innovation and business opportunities, as well as demonstrating commitment to the global problem of climatic change.

Pollution

From the outset, a Community policy has been concerned about pollution and the likely effects that **social dumping** has on fair trade between member states. The argument here is that if pollution controls in one member state are lax compared with those in another, then relative prices become distorted. The cost of producing goods in the country with lax controls would be lower because the cost of negative externalities is not taken into account. This would give a member state an unfair advantage if, in the other member state, the external costs of pollution had to be paid by the polluting business. (See Grant S., and Vidler C., *Heinemann Economics,* pp. 76–77.)

'Polluter pays' principle

The Community's Environmental Action Programme makes a firm commitment to the **'polluter pays' principle** (see box that follows). In the main, EU policy has used a whole raft of regulations to control polluting activities and has worked alongside the domestic policies of member states. In October 2005 the Commission also published important proposals for dealing with the ever-increasing environmental problems arising from the growth of air traffic. The background to this problem is that, unlike road transport where CO_2 emission levels are actually falling, this is not so for air transport. Other emissions, such as water vapour and aviation smog, as well as CO_2, are making ever-increasing contributions to the greenhouse effect and global warming. It is also the case that international aviation is excluded from the Kyoto Protocol.

A key issue is whether there should be a fixed energy tax on air tickets, or whether there should be some form of emissions trading as currently applies to energy-intensive industries such as iron and steel, electricity generation and cement production. There is also the problem of how this can be applied to non-EU airlines and services outside of the EU, as there is likely to be stiff opposition from US airlines especially. The benefit of an emission-trading scheme, as shown in the box, is that those airlines with newer, less polluting aeroplanes would of course pay less than airlines still using older, less fuel-efficient ones.

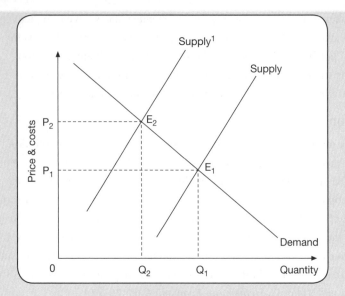

The above diagram shows that in a free market situation, Q_1 will be produced and the price charged will be P_1. If the social costs of production are taken into account, because the production of Q_1 involves polluting activities, then the supply curve shifts to the left. The new equilibrium E_2 is where Q_2 is the quantity produced and consumed, with the price charged now rising to P_2.

Output can be reduced in various ways including:

- regulations to restrict it to Q_2
- a green tax leading to a price rise to P_2
- tradeable permits to pollute, whereby those firms that want the right to pollute would have to pay a high and fair price to do so. Where a firm cuts pollution, it could sell its permit to pollute.

On the aviation issue, apart from opposition from one or two low-fare airlines, member states and most EU airline operators believe that the above proposals are acceptable, given the EU's firm commitment to sustainability.

Recycling

In a different environmental context, the recycling of tin cans, the EU and Germany have had a much publicised dispute. Here, the EU has argued that stringent German regulations are against the principles of the SEM (see box).

Environment 2010

The most recent EU environmental policy is an Action Programme entitled 'Environment 2010: Our future, our choice', covering a wide range of

Germany's tin can row

The European Commission has threatened to take legal action over the German government's controversial rubbish collection laws. In early 2003, Germany introduced a 0.2 euro deposit tax on certain types of canned drinks tin. To claim the deposit, once empty, customers must return the tin with proof of purchase to where it was bought.

Many consumers have stopped buying cans and some shops have stopped selling them, because of the additional inconvenience involved in handling returns. Hundreds of workers have lost their jobs. The Commission is concerned that this makes it more difficult for drinks companies to sell their products in Germany, and that it is against free market principles.

environmental issues. A particular focus of this latest Action Programme is on climate change and global warming (see earlier with respect to aviation). In addition it emphasises the importance of:

- enforcing existing environmental laws
- ensuring that environmental impact is taken into account in all relevant EU policies such as agriculture, fisheries, energy, transport and the internal market
- providing more information so that better choices can be made
- raising awareness over the importance of using land wisely
- involving businesses and consumers in putting forward relevant solutions to environmental problems.

The EU now has a much stronger profile in environmental matters. Many environmental issues transcend the EU's borders – acid rain, oil spills, hazardous waste, for example – and consequently, the EU has signed up to a range of international problems and conventions. Given the ever-growing concerns about climate change, it is very important that a combined EU policy transcends national policies as and where appropriate.

Summary

On completion of this chapter, you have learnt:

- that the EU has become increasingly active in working with national governments in some areas of policy
- why the funding of the EU budget is a contentious issue
- why the UK continues to take a 'wait and see' approach to EMU
- how the EU's Common Transport Policy has become an important facilitator for economic integration
- how regional policy is seeking to enhance the well-being of people in disadvantaged parts of the EU
- how the EU is trying to make a positive impact in the field of environmental policy

Further reading

Bamford, C. G., Chapters 1–6 *Transport Economics* (4th edition), Heinemann, 2006

Grant, S., Vidler, C., Sections 4.9 and 4.10 in *Heinemann Economics A2 for AQA*, Heinemann, 2003

Grant, S., Vidler, C., Sections 6.10 and 6.12 in *Heinemann Economics for OCR*, Heinemann, 2003

Useful websites

BBC news: www.bbc.co.uk

Europa: www.europa.eu.int

ECB: www.ecb.int

Activities

Topics for investigation

Obtain data on the economic performance of the UK economy and eurozone members such as France and Germany since the introduction of the single currency in 2002. Produce a brief economic report on the differences you have observed.

Exam-style practice questions

Data response question

Study the information contained in Figure 3.2 on page 40 and then answer the following questions:

1. a) What is meant by 'GDP per inhabitant (in PPS)' and why are differences in this measure an appropriate indicator of the regional problem. (4)

   b) Explain two limitations of the information contained in Figure 3.2. (4)

2. Compare variations in GDP per head between France and Germany. (4)

3. Comment on the policy implications of the variation in GDP per head in the UK. (8)

Essay questions

1. Use examples to analyse how the EU's policies complement those of the national governments of member states. (25)

2. Discuss whether it is appropriate for the EU to introduce a new environmental tax on air passenger travel. (25)

4 Producing in the EU

In this chapter you will learn:

- how the EU has realised the Single European Market (SEM)
- what are the benefits for trade and for businesses
- how firms have sought to improve their competitiveness as a result of the SEM
- why central and eastern European locations continue to attract manufacturing and certain types of service sector companies
- how the EU's Competition Policy is important in ensuring that the benefits of the SEM are not diluted.

> **Key words** Competition Commission • economies of scale
> methods of entry • merger • minimum efficient scale
> monopoly • non-tariff barriers • oligopoly • state aid
> unit labour costs

The Single European Market

During the early 1980s there was a growing sense of frustration because it was felt that the processes of economic integration were at a standstill and that Europe was lacking political vision and future direction. This was an emerging view as far as France and Germany were concerned; it was also the view of Jacques Delors who had become President of the European Commission in 1984.

The cause of these concerns was that the Treaty of Rome, with its so-called 'common market', remained an unfinished structure. More specifically, many **non-tariff barriers** (NTBs) hindered the free movement of goods, services, labour and capital. These NTBs took the form of a multitude of rules, regulations and fiscal measures that were applied individually by member states. Collectively, they were seen as holding back the completion of the common market.

The macroeconomic context is particularly relevant in two respects. First, Europe's principal economies were beginning to experience growing unemployment problems and very modest annual rates of growth compared to the USA, Japan and the emerging Asian 'tiger' economies. Second, as analysed later in Chapter 7, Europe was having to face up to the challenges and threats of globalisation. Japan especially was a powerful force in electronics, computer hardware, vehicle production and other high-technology sectors of manufacturing. Many of Japan's companies were well established and growing fast in Europe, particularly in the UK. The threat to Europe's competitiveness was serious. Against this background, Delors and others were concerned that Europe's leaders were squabbling among themselves over matters such as the EU budget and the CAP, when what they needed to address was how Europe as a whole could become more competitive in the global arena.

In the early to mid-1980s, the EU could hardly be described as '*Europe sans frontiers*' from a business standpoint. Some typical examples of NTBs were:

- frontier controls to ensure that imported goods complied with national regulations
- cabotage restrictions limiting the movement of goods by road by hauliers not based in a particular member state (see Chapter 3)
- problems for companies wishing to purchase a business or set up a new operation in another member state
- differences in professional and vocational qualifications and in social security systems that inhibited the flow of labour across the EU
- anti-competitive measures restricting which businesses could compete for public contracts and restricting entry into occupations as diverse as auctioneering and bookmaking.

The EU had tried to eliminate these NTBs long before the Single European Act of 1986 – the problem was that little progress had been made, largely because of the protective attitude of member states who could veto any moves by the Commission that were thought to be against their own economic interests.

The Single European Act, therefore, sought to revisit the Treaty of Rome and create the SEM. It stated: 'The internal market shall comprise an area without internal frontiers in which the free movement of goods, persons, services and capital is ensured.'

A target date of 1 January 1993 was set, by which time around 300 directives had to be passed and incorporated into the national laws of member states. No mean task, to say the least!

The SEM is based on the 'four freedoms', namely eliminating in full, not just reducing, obstacles to the free movement of goods, people, businesses and services.

More specifically this involves the following.

- Goods. Any EU-based company can sell any of their products anywhere in the EU. In turn, consumers can buy anything they want anywhere within the EU at a fair price.

- People. Any EU citizen can live and work in any member state. Educational and professional qualifications must be fully recognised. Social security and healthcare systems must not mitigate against this mobility.
- Businesses. Currency and business capital can flow freely between member states. Any EU business can access financial services in any member state. There should be no discrimination against businesses in one member state wishing to enter markets in another member state, either through purchasing an established company or in setting up a new 'greenfield' operation.
- Services. All types of financial and professional service can be offered in any member state by any business based in any other member state.

By the end of 1992, only 95 per cent of the 300 directives required to complete the SEM had been launched; just over 20 per cent had not been put into practice. In the years from 1993, virtually all of these directives have now become law.

Benefits of the single market

The completion (or more correctly, near completion) of the SEM has created a huge wider market. Initially this market had 380 million consumers, but with the EU25, this has increased to around 450 million consumers. This in itself has resulted in substantial change, particularly as far as EU businesses are concerned. The macroeconomic effects can be seen through:

- an acceleration in the growth of intra-EU trade and increased competitiveness in external trade
- an increase in internal and external investment as a result of realising the benefits of being able to invest in a single market.

Both of these benefits are analysed in Chapter 7.

At a microeconomic level, the SEM has had an important effect on market structures and on the restructuring of industrial production. To all intents and purposes, the SEM as its name indicates is a domestic market for EU-based firms. This was most certainly not the case when there were hundreds of NTBs mitigating against free trade between member states. For companies, the SEM gives scope to increase their output and, very significantly, to benefit from greater **economies of scale**. For consumers, this has meant lower prices due to the increased level of competition. This benefit of the SEM is particularly evident in the European motor manufacturing and assembly industry.

The box below shows how, in theory, as the scale of production increases, long-run average costs fall. Possible sources of internal economies of scale are:

- bulk buying of components from suppliers
- the automation of vehicle assembly to reduce labour costs
- European-wide marketing campaigns, promoting the same models across member states
- concentration of production on a limited range of vehicle models, so that factories can specialise.

Economies of scale in car manufacturing

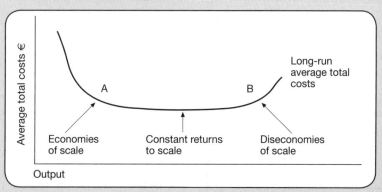

Over the short run period, a car manufacturer cannot adjust the number or size of its factories. Variations in production, in response to changes in demand, can only be made through changing the input of variable factors of production, such as labour and vehicle parts. The cost of its factories is therefore a fixed cost in the short run.

Over time, the manufacturer can expand the size of its factories, build new ones or close old ones. The cost of factories therefore becomes a variable cost in the long run. The completion of the SEM has resulted in a situation where to remain competitive, the **minimum efficient scale** has increased. This is represented between points A and B on the above diagram. Empirical studies have put this level of output as high as 200 000 vehicles per year. So, to remain competitive, there are market pressures on firms to rationalise production into a smaller number of high-tech production units that serve a wide geographical market within the EU, and where each unit produces a very limited range of models.

A consequence of the competitive need to benefit from economies of scale has been a rationalisation of ownership of European-based car manufacturers (see Figure 4.1). The main features are:

- the strength of German[h] (VW, BMW especially) and French-owned (PSA and Renault) manufacturers
- US-owned manufacturers of established European marques (GM and Ford).

Asian-owned producers such as Toyota, Honda and Nissan are not shown in Figure 4.1, although all are important producers in the European market.

Consumers have benefited from these changes. For the EU12, price transparency has resulted in a highly competitive market. Cross-border transactions have become increasingly common. However, it is still by no means easy for UK consumers to purchase right-hand drive vehicles elsewhere in the EU, mainly due to the uncompetitive practices of manufacturers and dealers. Although new car prices in the UK have fallen in recent years due to increased competition, they remain the highest of any EU12 member state.

Changes in the EU car manufacturing industry have not necessarily been beneficial to the UK economy as a whole. For example, in recent years, Ford

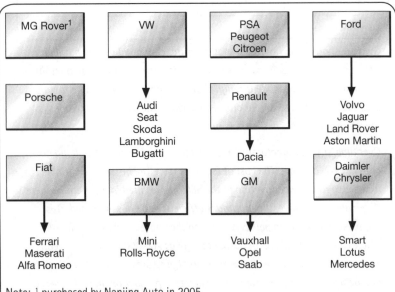

Note: [1] purchased by Nanjing Auto in 2005
      [2] excludes non-European companies such as Toyota, Nissan and Honda that have assembly plants in Europe

Figure 4.1: Principal European-based car manufacturers in 2003[2]

has stopped production at its Dagenham factory, MG Rover ceased production at Longbridge, Birmingham in 2005, and in April 2006, PSA announced the closure of its Peugeot plant in Coventry. The loss of this capacity can be largely blamed on the reality of the economics of car manufacturing in the single market.

On a less specific level, other business sectors such as food manufacturing, pharmaceuticals, transport and grocery retailing have experienced similar changes in market structure to those described above for car manufacturing. The general benefits can be summarised as being:

- increased scale of operations and benefits from economies of scale
- the mutual recognition of products, leading to greater standardisation within the SEM
- concentration of production at fewer sites, as there is no longer a need for many firms to have production plants in each of the main member states (reduced distribution costs have also been a contributory factor)
- less administration through the general use of the Single Administration Document (SAD).

At the same time, it must be remembered that EU firms continue to face increasing competition from non-EU companies that have sought to gain the same range of benefits by setting up their business in the EU. The realisation of the SEM has therefore created a highly competitive business environment for all concerned.

Producing and doing business in the New Member States

Long before their accession in May 2004, companies were queuing up to invest in manufacturing and service sector activity in the NMS. Poland, the Czech Republic, Hungary and Slovakia have been the main recipients of this form of FDI, estimated to be over US$100 billion since the fall of the Berlin Wall in 1989. Global industries, led by motor vehicle manufacturers, have created new bases for industrial production, invariably replacing former state-owned operations. In turn, this investment has acted as a catalyst for local enterprise – an estimated 5 million companies have been established over the past fifteen years. Most of course remain very small, but they have become important providers of huge supplies of parts, semi-finished products and services to foreign companies.

The box opposite shows four of the most successful EU-owned companies to penetrate the CEE market. In all cases, they saw the potential business opportunities around the time of the Treaty of Copenhagen (1993), in which

EU leaders agreed in principle to accession requests from former Communist countries in central and eastern Europe. Full membership for the NMS provides a new starting point for further investment, and much potential remains for foreign-owned as well as domestic businesses in this part of the EU.

There are various **methods of entry** into this market. These are through:

- the direct purchase of a manufacturing or service sector businesses; many such sales have been of former state-run companies, consistent with policies of privatisation
- joint ventures, where foreign companies provide much needed business capital to fund modernisation and expansion; in many respects, this is less risky than outright purchase
- setting up a new 'greenfield' operation in order to gain new market access from a location that is determined by the investing business
- franchising of a particular product or business concept to new 'local' providers. This has been particularity prevalent in retailing and fast food markets. Typical examples are Benetton, The Body Shop, McDonald's, Pizza Hut and Kentucky Fried Chicken.

The first three methods of entry clearly involve more risk than franchising, where the franchisee normally has to make an up-front payment before it is able to sell the products concerned in its own market. The highest level of risk is where there is a **merger** or acquisition, although this form of market entry offers immediate access for an outsider business into a new market. This method has successfully been applied by manufacturing companies and retailers (see box).

A presence in the NMS has many existing and potential attractions. These include the following.

- Lower **unit labour costs**. As shown in Table 4.1, unit labour costs in the NMS are much lower than elsewhere in the EU. This has been a main reason why German companies have transferred production to locations in central and eastern Europe, finding it more economic to then supply their domestic and other markets from these lower cost locations.
- A supportive business environment. National and regional governments and trade unions have invariably been very keen to see new job opportunities created in areas that have experienced increased unemployment during the transition period to full EU membership.
- Rising living standards. As analysed in Chapter 3, although living standards in the largest NMS are well below the EU average, they have been growing steadily in recent years. Economic growth rates of at least double those of the EU15 have been recorded and can be expected to

Four western companies doing good business in Eastern Europe

Volkswagen

One of the first, and now the largest motor producer in the region, with factories in the Czech Republic (Skoda, 100 per cent) and Poland (Skoda AUTO Polska 51 per cent).

Increasing output of high-end vehicles such as the Toureg SUV in Slovakia and the Audi sports car in Hungary.

RZB Group

Austrian bank with regional network in fifteen ex-Communist states; last year made 70 per cent of group profits in eastern Europe, highest proportion for any large EU-listed company. Retains pioneering spirit, buying control last year of a bank in Berlarus. Total assets in EU accession countries (Hungary, Slovak Republic, Czech Republic, Poland, Slovenia): € 10.7bn. Total employees: 7 196.

Tesco

British supermarket chain which has become the leading hypermarket retailer in eastern Europe. Tesco has £1.5bn invested in European accession countries (Poland, Hungary, Slovak Republic and Czech Republic), with 38 000 regional employees and 83 stores. Continues to invest £250m annually in the region.

Deutsche Telekom

German telecommunications operator. Biggest investor in east European telecoms; owns controlling stakes in Matav (59.5 per cent) and Slovak Telekom (51 per cent), Hungarian and Slovak telecoms networks; investments in Croatia (51 per cent stake in Hrvatske telekomunikacije), Poland (49 per cent in Polska Telefonia Cyfrowa), and the Czech Republic (T-Mobile Czech Republic 60.8 per cent); rumoured interest in investing in Cesky Telecom, Czech former monopoly. Employees in the companies above: 39 152.

Source: *Financial Times*, 27 April 2004 (adaptation)

persist for some time. Consequently, an increasing number of consumers have more discretionary income to spend on non-essential grocery products and on a range of consumer goods such as cars, electronics products and fashion clothing.

Table 4.1: Average labour costs per hour[1] ($US) in 2003

Country	Labour cost per hour	Country	Labour cost per hour
Germany	30.86	Hungary	3.80
France	21.53	Czech Republic	3.39
UK	19.24	Poland	3.14
Spain	14.94	Slovakia	2.15

[1] includes time worked and employer expenditure on insurance programmes and labour taxes for all types of employment

Source: Economist Intelligence Unit

Car manufacturing and assembly firms have been at the forefront of the push to invest in Poland, Hungary, the Czech Republic and Slovakia. Prior to these countries becoming full members of the EU, VW and Fiat were the first European companies to see the business opportunities of purchasing undercapitalised, moribund manufacturers in these countries. Domestic markets in the NMS8 are running at around 600 000 vehicles per annum, with projected rises of 10 per cent per annum.

More recently, US and Asian manufacturers have entered these markets, producing relatively low-cost models for distribution to the EU market as a whole. The major concerns of these manufacturers are rising living standards causing rapid wage inflation, and the cost of importing from suppliers in the West.

Service sector companies have also used the continuing economic integration in Europe to extend their businesses into the NMS. The case of Tesco has already been mentioned. In addition, French and German grocery retailers have penetrated central European markets as shown in Figure 4.2.

Their motives for this type of expansion are in some respects the same as for manufacturing companies, namely to gain market share in countries with rising living standards and high projected income growth. A further consideration is that in their home markets, the extent of their market shares is reaching a saturation level beyond which these companies are increasingly likely to attract the attention of their respective competition authorities and the EC's **Competition Commission**.

Multinational hotel chains have also successfully set up in most NMS8 markets. Typical of these are the Marriott, Hilton, Holiday Inn and Novotel

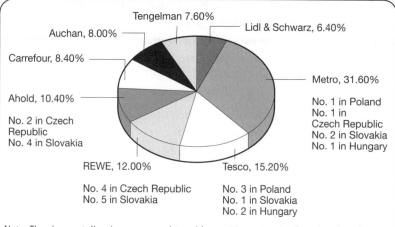

Tengelman 7.60%
Lidl & Schwarz, 6.40%
Auchan, 8.00%
Carrefour, 8.40%
Metro, 31.60%
Ahold, 10.40%
No. 1 in Poland
No. 1 in
Czech Republic
No. 2 in Slovakia
No. 1 in Hungary
No. 2 in Czech
Republic
No. 4 in Slovakia
REWE, 12.00%
Tesco, 15.20%
No. 4 in Czech Republic
No. 5 in Slovakia
No. 3 in Poland
No. 1 in Slovakia
No. 2 in Hungary

Note: The above retailers have managed to achieve a 25 per cent total market share in the four central European economies of Poland, Czech Republic, Slovakia and Hungary. The remaining 75 per cent of the market is with domestic grocery retailers in these countries.

Figure 4.2: Relative shares of foreign retailers' grocery sales in four central European economies in 2003 (%)

brands. The market for business travellers is growing fast, and particularly in capital cities, there are growing numbers of tourists from the rest of the EU. This growth has been helped through the ever-expanding network of low-cost airline routes (see Chapter 3).

The expansion of foreign-owned manufacturing and retail businesses into central and eastern Europe has in turn created new market opportunities for logistics companies to provide supply chain management services. In many cases, these specialist companies are working with the same clients, and providing very similar services, to their operations in the UK, France and Germany. The UK's Exel, now part of Deutshe Post World Net, has been a leading provider for many years. Other important players are Faure et Machet, Frans-Maas, Schenkers, Giraud and Norbert Dentressangle. In addition, joint ventures have been set up with domestic providers of transport services in Poland and the Czech Republic especially.

Competition policy and the Single European Market

As analysed at the start of this chapter, the SEM is underpinned by the four freedoms. In particular, the removal of NTBs has made the European market more competitive and, as shown later, has created new opportunities for companies in both the EU15 and NMS. For these processes to work efficiently and effectively, it is essential that businesses throughout the EU are able to compete on a fair basis. Only in this way can the full economic and social benefits of the SEM be realised. It is the function of EU Competition Policy to ensure that these important principles are protected and upheld. Its rationale lies very much in the economics of market structures. A summary of some key points is given below. (For more details see Griffiths, A. and Ison, S., *Business Economics*, pp. 31–82.)

Economic theory maintains the following.

- Competition produces the best allocation of resources in a market; competitive markets are 'good'.
- A perfectly competitive market is the only one that is productively and allocatively efficient. All other market structures are relatively inefficient.
- Under a **monopoly**, prices are higher and output is lower than in perfect competition. Monopolists are able to earn supernormal profits in the long run. An exception might be state-owned monopolies, although these are criticised for being x-inefficient.
- An **oligopoly** is a market structure with a small number of large firms that are protected by high barriers to entry. Interdependence is a key feature.
- Branding, product differentiation and advertising are the main ways in which businesses compete. In principle, collusion over price or output is possible, though illegal.

Pure monopolies are rare. About the only realistic European examples are state-owned. Privatisation has reduced their numbers considerably, although in some cases arguably detrimental private sector monopolies have replaced them. Oligopoly is much more the norm in many manufacturing markets. Typical examples are car manufacturing, aerospace, many types of food and drink production, electrical products and electronics manufacturing. In the service sector, examples are grocery retailing, telecommunications, banking and logistics.

National governments of member states have their own policies to avert the power of such businesses in their domestic markets. The EU's role is to complement these policies, specifically to prevent any activities that inhibit competition within the SEM as a whole. Figure 4.3 shows the three main pillars of Competition Policy.

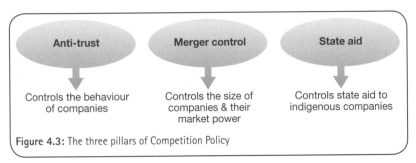

Figure 4.3: The three pillars of Competition Policy

Anti-trust

This is a conventional objective of any type of competition policy and relates back to the potential behaviour of monopolists and oligopolists. The EU's role is to intervene where restrictive agreements and other practices inhibit competition in markets. Typical examples might be if it can be proven that oligopolists collude to fix prices, or have an agreement to not compete with each other in a particular market. A producer's cartel might also restrict output to increase prices. Other actions could be against a monopolist that abuses its power by fixing high prices or using illegal tactics to keep potential competitors out of a market. There are many examples of cases where the Commission has fined companies for acting as cartels and infringing competition rules. A particularly controversial and public case has been that of price fixing by up-market German car manufacturers to prevent competition between authorised dealers. The EU has also sought to create conditions that allow dealers to sell several makes of cars with a view to increasing price competition.

Merger control

This aspect of competition policy is designed to ensure that acquisitions and mergers do not seriously reduce competition in a market, and result in a situation where a technical monopoly is created. In this field, the EU has been particularly concerned about increasing concentration in the energy sector through amalgamations and the merger of gas and electricity companies. This is seen as being counter to the creation of an integrated energy market across the whole of the EU, where firms are engaged in cross-boarder competition.

State aid

The aim here is for there to be effective limits to the subsidies that are provided to ailing manufacturing companies, as well as to new investors in member states. It is argued that such handouts by national regional and local governments allow recipient companies to be protected from competition. A recent high profile case has been the subsidies that were being given to Ryanair by Charleroi airport in Belgium. On a wider scale, it is for this reason that the UK government was unable to intervene in the collapse of MG Rover and the closure of Peugeot's Coventry factory.

In practice, the EU's Competition Policy is very complex. It is also a very active area of policy, with many annual notifications and complaints, some of which result in investigations and decisions by the Commission. It may not appear to be a very important area of policy, largely because it does not attract the media coverage of other common policies. The reality is that an effective Competition Policy is at the heart of the SEM and essential for upholding the wider competitiveness of EU firms in their own, as well as in global markets.

Summary

On completion of this chapter you have learnt that:

- the removal of hundreds of non-tariff barriers has been necessary for the completion of the SEM
- this in turn has led to an acceleration in intra-EU trade and increased competitiveness for EU firms
- the SEM can provide firms with benefits from economies of scale
- a location in central and eastern Europe can be very beneficial for certain types of manufacturing and service sector businesses
- if unchecked, monopolies and oligopolies can erode the benefits of the SEM
- EU Competition Policy seeks to control their activities, and their size; it also controls the aid that can be given to businesses.

Further reading

Grant, S., Vidler, C., Section 4.3 in *Heinemann Economics A2 for AQA*, Heinemann, 2003

Grant, S., Vidler, C., Section 6.4 in *Heinemann Economics for OCR*, Heinemann, 2003

Griffiths, A., Ison, S., Chapters 2–6 in *Studies in Economics and Business: Business Economics*, Heinemann, 2001

Useful websites

EU: www.europa.eu.int/comm/competition

Activities

Topics for investigation

Use the Internet to find examples of:

- EU manufacturing companies that have closed their operations in the EU15 and moved to one of the NMS
- non-EU manufacturing companies that have set up in the NMS.

Discuss the economic motives for these location decisions.

Exam-style practice questions

Data response question

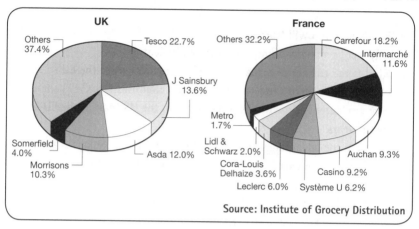

UK

Others 37.4%
Tesco 22.7%
J Sainsbury 13.6%
Asda 12.0%
Morrisons 10.3%
Somerfield 4.0%

France

Others 32.2%
Carrefour 18.2%
Intermarché 11.6%
Auchan 9.3%
Casino 9.2%
Système U 6.2%
Leclerc 6.0%
Cora-Louis Delhaize 3.6%
Lidl & Schwarz 2.0%
Metro 1.7%

Source: Institute of Grocery Distribution

1. The pie charts show the market shares in the UK and France. Compare the market concentrations of grocery retailing in France and the UK in 2004. (10)

2. Comment on whether the following are likely to be concerned with level of market concentration:

   a) the competition authorities in France and the UK

   b) the EU's Competition Commission. (15)

Essay questions

1. Explain how the completion of the Single Market has benefited:

   a) EU firms; b) EU consumers; c) The EU economy as a whole. (25)

2. a) Use a diagram to compare the long-run equilibrium of a monopolist with that of firms in a perfectly competitive market. (10)

   b) Discuss the extent to which this comparison might lead you to conclude that 'monopolies are bad, competition is good'. (15)

3. a) Explain why the EU needs a Competition Policy. (10)

   b) Comment on how such a policy interacts with the competition policies of the EU's member states. (15)

5 Working in the EU

In this chapter you will learn:

- why labour markets do not often work efficiently
- what is the current principal cause of unemployment in the EU
- how unemployment rates vary between EU countries
- why productivity growth has been higher in the US than in the EU in recent years
- what are the advantages and disadvantages of a flexible labour market
- how the EU influences working hours and working conditions
- how minimum wages vary across the EU
- what limits the migration of workers within the EU
- what are the key characteristics of the three main EU labour market models.

> **Key words** cyclical unemployment • flexible labour market
> labour market failure • Lisbon strategy • minimum wages
> participation rate • productivity • structural unemployment

Introduction

The pay workers receive, the working conditions they face, and indeed their chances of gaining employment vary both within EU member countries and across the EU.

Workers' experiences and countries' macroeconomic performance would clearly benefit from a well-performing labour market. What is more controversial is what constitutes a well-performing labour market, and what the best policies are to achieve it. In comparing the performance of the labour markets in the different member countries of the EU, it is useful to consider a range of aspects including unemployment, productivity, flexibility, working hours and conditions, **minimum wages** and migration.

Labour market failure

Labour market failure is clearly undesirable. It occurs when labour markets fail to allocate and use labour efficiently. The most obvious sign of this is unemployment. Other signs include workers being in jobs they are not best suited to, being paid above or below their marginal revenue **productivity**, under-provision of training and a lack of skilled workers.

There are a number of causes of labour market failure. Workers and employers may lack information, such as on job vacancies and where the most skilled workers are to be found. There may be dominant sellers of labour (trade unions) and dominant buyers of labour who distort the wage rate paid. Some workers may be discriminated against. Training is a merit good and so may be under-consumed and under-provided. Labour is also frequently immobile, both occupationally and geographically.

The Treaty of Rome outlines the EU's ambition to have a well-performing labour market that minimises labour market failure. It expects member countries to contribute to a high level of employment and to promote a skilled, trained and adaptable labour force.

Unemployment

Unemployment is a waste of labour resources which results in forgone output and can impose significant costs on those unemployed. It can be caused by a lack of aggregate demand. This type of unemployment, known as **cyclical unemployment**, arises when the economy operates below full capacity and there is a negative output gap as shown in Figure 5.1.

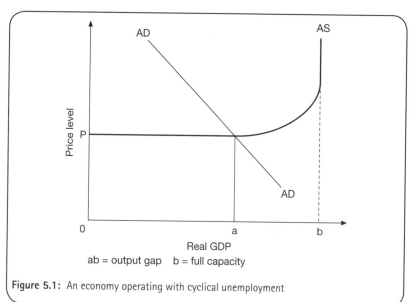

Figure 5.1: An economy operating with cyclical unemployment

Unemployment may also be caused by problems on the supply side. There may be job vacancies, but the unemployed may lack the information, skills or willingness to fill them, or they may live in different areas. This type of unemployment is called **structural unemployment**.

Some of the current EU unemployment is cyclical. It has resulted from a slowdown in economic growth in a number of member countries, including Germany and Italy. A slower increase in aggregate demand may result in actual economic growth being below potential (trend) economic growth. Fewer workers would then be needed as improvements in technology and increases in productivity enable firms to produce a slightly higher output with a smaller labour force.

Most of current EU unemployment, however, is thought to be of a structural nature, arising from occupational and geographical immobility, lack of incentives to work and lack of adaptability.

Figure 5.2 shows the EU labour market. There is unemployment of xz amount; xy of this is cyclical and yz is structural, with the aggregate labour force (ALF) being greater than those able and willing to work at the going wage rate, i.e. the aggregate supply of labour (ASL).

The extent of unemployment varies across the EU. Table 5.1 shows that in 2005, Ireland had the lowest rate of unemployment, based on the International Labour Organization (ILO) measure, and Poland had the highest rate.

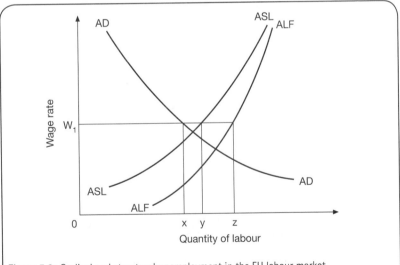

Figure 5.2: Cyclical and structural unemployment in the EU labour market

Table 5.1: Unemployment rates in EU member states in 2005

	%		%
Austria	4.5	Latvia	9.6
Belgium	8.0	Lithuania	9.1
Cyprus	5.6	Luxembourg	4.4
Czech Republic	8.3	Malta	6.9
Denmark	5.1	Netherlands	4.7
Estonia	8.1	Poland	18.2
Finland	8.9	Portugal	6.9
France	9.7	Slovakia	16.5
Germany	9.6	Slovenia	5.8
Greece	10.5	Spain	10.3
Hungary	6.3	Sweden	6.1
Ireland	4.3	UK	4.6
Italy	7.8		

Source: infoBase Europe Factsheet No. 078

Employment participation

In addition to differences in unemployment, there are also differences in
participation rates. Italy has a relatively low participation rate. In 2005,
62 per cent of Italian people of working age were either in employment or
seeking employment. In contrast, the UK has a high participation rate, with
83.4 per cent of men and 73.6 per cent of women in the labour force in 2005.
It is interesting to note, however, that while female economic activity is rising
in the UK, male economic activity is declining.

In 2000 the EU adopted a reform agenda known as the **Lisbon strategy**,
designed to make it the world's most dynamic and competitive economy by
2010. The EU wants to raise its trend growth rate to 3 per cent by, among
other ways, increasing participation rates among those aged 55–64 years.

Productivity

Another labour market goal of the Lisbon strategy is to raise productivity
growth. For some time EU productivity growth has been below that of
the US. There are also variations between EU countries with, for instance,

productivity growth being more rapid in France than the UK and Italy's productivity even falling in recent years – see Table 5.2.

Table 5.2: A comparison between productivity growth in selected EU countries and the US

1994 = 100 (base year)					
	USA	France	Germany	Italy	UK
2001	113.4	107.6	108.9	107.9	113.7
2002	115.6	108.2	109.6	106.8	115.2
2003	117.7	109.4	110.5	106.2	116.9
2004	121.3	111.7	111.3	105.6	119.7

Source: Table 13, *National Institute Economic Review* No. 194, October 2005

The main reason US workers enjoy higher disposable incomes and so higher material living standards than their EU counterparts is their higher productivity (although care has to be taken in making comparisons). If productivity continues to grow more rapidly in the US, the difference in living standards will widen. More spare capacity will be created in the US economy, allowing it to grow faster.

Why has productivity growth been higher in the USA than in the EU in recent years? One reason is that US businesses have invested more heavily in ICT equipment than EU businesses in the 1990s and the first decade of the 2000s. More capital per worker, referred to as capital deepening, and capital embodying more advanced technology does not in itself guarantee higher output per worker. The workers have to possess the necessary skills to use the capital to its full potential.

Unfortunately the UK has something of a skills disadvantage. It has a relatively high proportion of workers who lack basic skills. Indeed in 2005, Latvia was the only EU country with a worse standard of workplace literacy. The UK also has a lower proportion of its labour force with intermediate skills (A level or vocational equivalent) and above than the US, France and Germany.

A more skilled labour force enables an economy not only to reap the full advantage of advances in technology and net investment, but also to make more efficient use of existing resources of capital and labour. The latter is sometimes referred to as multifactor productivity growth.

The two main measures of productivity are output per worker and output per worker hour. The government and the Federal Reserve base their measures on output in the non-farm business sector – they do not count agricultural and public sector output. In contrast, the European Central Bank (ECB) and most EU national governments measure output per worker in the whole economy. This difference tends to overstate US productivity relative to EU productivity, as the public sector often has relatively slow productivity growth.

Flexibility

A **flexible labour market** is one that adjusts smoothly and quickly to changes in demand and supply conditions. This adjustment can take place through changes in wages and/or employment. In the latter case there may be alterations in the number of workers employed, the hours they work, the time they work, the type of work they do and where they do it.

Flexible working can allow firms to match production closely to demand and thereby keep average costs low. It can also benefit workers. For instance, some workers may want to work overtime and some may wish to go part-time. In addition, a flexible labour market may in the long run generate more employment. This is because firms are more likely to recruit more staff during periods of high demand if they know that they can dismiss them quickly and with little cost should demand fall in the future. Such flexibility, however, can also bring disadvantages for workers. They may face more insecurity, greater pressure to be adaptable and be subject to periods of unemployment. There is also more wage inequality in a flexible market.

The UK is considered to have a more flexible labour market than most of its fellow EU member states, particularly France, Germany and Italy. A study by the European Foundation for the Improvement of Living and Working Conditions published in 2006 reported that the top four EU countries, in terms of the percentage of employers operating flexible hours, were Latvia, Sweden, Finland and the UK. The UK actually came top when it came to allowing workers to switch easily from full-time to part-time work. It did, however, come lower down in terms of offering a range of flexible working arrangements. One of these is what is known as working time accounts. These permit workers to build up hours that can be used later to take time off in compensation.

There are a number of factors that may reduce labour market flexibility. These include taxes on employing labour, minimum wages, generous employment benefits and employment protection legislation.

Within the eurozone, flexibility is thought to be particularly important. This is because a member country can no longer respond to an economic shock which hits it harder than the other members by cutting the rate of interest or devaluing its currency to raise aggregate demand and increase its international competitiveness. In such a situation, unemployment will rise unless wages fall or unemployed workers move to areas where there are vacancies.

Globalisation is also putting pressure on all the EU25 economies to be more flexible. It could be argued, however, that due to the greater volatility and insecurity globalisation generates, it creates more need for social protection, which can reduce flexibility.

Employment protection legislation

Employment protection legislation can place a number of requirements on employers, such as having to give a period of notice before dismissing workers and giving workers the right to appeal against unfair dismissal. Such protection makes it more expensive to hire and fire workers. It provides more security for those in work but can make it more difficult for the unemployed to find jobs. This can create an insider/outsider labour market problem. Those who have jobs benefit from the protection and are likely to resist any attempts to reduce that protection.

Working hours and conditions

The hours and conditions workers face can have a significant impact on their quality of life. They also influence both the total amount workers produce and their productivity.

Long working hours and good working conditions should mean relatively high output. Long hours, however, can reduce productivity. Working for long hours at a stretch may mean that workers become tired. As a result they may produce less output per hour, suffer more periods of sickness, and the quality of both their work and family life may suffer.

The EU's 48-hour Working Time Directive proposed a limit of 48 hours (including overtime) on the working week, minimum rest breaks during work and four weeks' annual paid holiday. Most members adopted it in full in 1993 although a few exempted some specific sectors. The UK initially refused to adopt it. The government at the time argued that it was important, in the face of growing global competition, for workers to be free to work longer hours if necessary to meet orders. In 1998 it did adopt it with certain exemptions and with the provision that individual workers should be allowed to work longer should they wish. The UK government extended the regulations to junior doctors in 2004 and to haulage drivers in 2005.

The UK government has now adopted many of the aspects of the Social Charter (see Chapter 3). For instance, it introduced a national minimum wage in 1997, implemented the EU works council directive in 1998 and its parental leave directive in 1999. It is also following the EU's Employment Directive of 2000 for tackling age discrimination. The UK is due to introduce legislation in October 2006 making it illegal to discriminate against anyone because of their age when they apply for a job, training or courses in further/higher education. The member states have also agreed two targets to achieve by 2010:

- at least half the EU population aged between 55 and 64 years should be in employment
- there should be a five-year increase in the average age at which people withdraw from the labour force.

If the EU is successful in meeting these targets, there will be an increase of 5 million older workers in the EU15. This will increase the productive potential of the EU and make pension provision more sustainable.

The UK government has, however, opposed the EU's attempt to introduce a law strengthening the rights of Europe's temporary workers. This was designed to give temporary workers the same pay and conditions as permanent staff, including holiday pay, after they had been with a firm for six weeks. The UK, Denmark, Germany and Ireland argued that the move would reduce flexibility in the labour market. The UK was particularly worried as it employs two-thirds of all EU temporary workers.

Minimum wages

Most, but not all, of the EU25 have national minimum wages, enforced by law. In those which do not, such as Sweden, minimum wages are effectively set by collective bargaining agreements.

Governments set minimum wages to protect those workers with weak bargaining power and to reduce poverty. Economists, however, disagree about the effects of minimum wages. Some argue that a national minimum wage increases the cost of labour and so reduces employment. Others claim that it counters monopsony power (buying power) in the labour market and can raise employment by increasing aggregate demand and raising productivity, through increasing workers' motivation and reducing labour turnover. Figure 5.3 shows the introduction of a national minimum wage increasing both the pay of the low paid and their employment, as a result of the rising demand for labour.

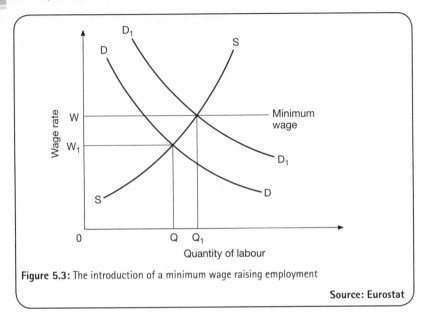

Figure 5.3: The introduction of a minimum wage raising employment

Source: Eurostat

Obviously, the impact that a national minimum wage has depends crucially on where it is set. Indeed if it is set below the market equilibrium level it will have no effect.

Member countries' minimum wages vary, as shown in Figure 4.

Figure 5.4 shows that in 2004, Lithuania had the lowest minimum wage of the EU25 at €121 and Luxembourg the highest at €1 403. Romania and Bulgaria's minimum wages were even lower.

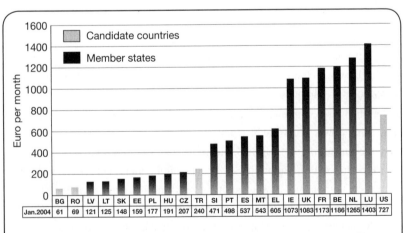

Figure 5.4: Minimum wages in EU member states, candidate countries and the USA, January 2004, euro

Source: Eurostat

The minimum wage as a proportion of average monthly gross earnings also differs, but in the majority of cases it is below 50 per cent. Ireland's minimum wage was 50 per cent of average monthly earnings in 2004, and the only member country where it was above 50 per cent was Malta, at 54 per cent.

Intra-EU migration

It might be expected that workers would move from EU member countries with low wages and high unemployment to those with high wages and labour shortages. Such a movement could be anticipated to narrow wage differentials between the countries. In fact, although there is some migration within the EU, it is less than would be expected. What causes this geographical immobility? The reasons include family ties, language and cultural barriers, and lack of information on rights, opportunities, wages and working conditions in other member countries.

The European Employment Services (EES) is a European labour market network for cooperation among state and private sector employer organisations and trade unions. It runs a labour market database that provides information to both employers and workers about labour market conditions and opportunities in other member countries.

A barrier to labour mobility, however, was placed on the NMS on their entry in 2004, as mentioned in Chapter 2. Fear of the impact on unemployment levels, wage rates and benefits in their countries led most of the EU15 countries to impose a time limit before NMS workers will be at full liberty to work anywhere in the EU.

Those countries, including the UK, that are allowing free entry of workers from the NMS are reaping a number of benefits (see box). For example, UK

Immigrants have boosted UK growth

About 300 000 citizens of the ten countries who joined the EU in 2004 have taken up new jobs in the UK. New research by Ernst & Young Item Club shows one in three immigrants into the UK from 'new Europe' are taking up office management posts, paying £300 million into the treasury in 2006 alone.

The report calculates the new workforce will boost UK growth by 0.2 per cent in 2006 and 0.4 per cent in 2007, while keeping interest and inflation rates low and easing the pensions burden. The UK workforce has also become younger and more flexible.

Source: *The Independent*, 25 May 2006 (adaptation)

bus companies, unable to recruit UK bus drivers, have avoided having to cancel services by employing Polish bus drivers, some of whom had been made redundant as a result of Poland's privatisation and deregulation of its bus services. Employers have found many migrant workers to be more prepared than UK workers to work long hours and, in some cases, to accept minimum wages or just above minimum wages.

The ability to draw on labour from eastern Europe to fill vacancies has caused some unions to express concerns that immigration is depressing wage rises in the UK. If, however, it strengthens the UK economy, it may enable output and incomes to rise more rapidly. It is also interesting to note that with ageing populations in much of Europe, Japan and the USA, there may be more competition for workers in the future.

EU versus US labour markets

The EU or, as it is sometimes called, the European labour market model, is characterised as relatively inflexible, immobile and inefficient. Most EU member countries are seen as placing a high weight on social justice and cohesion and have extensive welfare safety nets for vulnerable groups.

In contrast, the US labour market is perceived as having a relatively high degree of flexibility and mobility. It does, however, provide less support for vulnerable groups. The welfare system is less developed, there is more reliance on individual responsibilities, and income is more unevenly distributed. Workers in the US are more likely to experience unemployment than their EU counterparts, often at very short notice. However any such unemployment is likely to be for a shorter time than will be experienced in the EU.

These two models highlight the possible conflict between social cohesion and efficiency. It is, however, a somewhat simplistic view. In the EU there is actually more than one labour market model. Two of these models seek to combine social cohesion and efficiency. Table 5.3 compares some of the main characteristics of the Continental, Nordic and Anglo-Saxon models.

The Continental model

The Continental model is said to be relatively inflexible, with too much state regulation and too high taxes. The French government, for example, protects its workers from the consequences of the market to a large extent. Public sector workers, accounting for nearly 40 per cent of all workers, effectively have jobs for life unless they commit gross misconduct. Workers in both the private and public sectors enjoy short working days, long holidays and retire early.

In 2006, the French government did seek to introduce more flexibility in a bid to reduce unemployment among young workers. Its youth unemployment was high and increasing at the time, with one in four young French people being out of work. The prime minister, Dominique de Villepin, wanted to introduce a new form of work contract which would have allowed employers to hire workers between the ages of eighteen and 26 on two-year contracts. At the end of these contracts, employers would be free to dismiss any workers they did not want to keep.

It was hoped that this measure, by making it easier and cheaper to hire and fire young workers, would encourage French firms to employ more young workers. However, this proposed withdrawal of job protection for young workers provoked fierce opposition, with student and trade unions demonstrating in the streets. In response to these protests, President Chirac first revised the proposal, reducing the duration of the contract to one year, and then withdrew it altogether.

Table 5.3: European Labour Market Models

	Continental model	Nordic model	Anglo-Saxon model
Examples	Austria, France & Germany	Denmark, Finland & Sweden	Ireland & UK
Level of government intervention	high	high	low
Power of trade unions	high	high	low
Regulations on dismissals	high	average	low
Minimum wages	high	high	high
Unemployment benefits	generous	generous but short term	not very generous
Unemployment rate	relatively high	low	low
Employment rate	relatively low	high	high
Duration of unemployment	tends to be long term	short term	short term
Average no. of hours worked	low & inflexible	relatively high	high & flexible
Sense of job security	high	relatively high	low
Labour market efficiency	low	high	high
Income equality	high	high	low
Priority	social cohesion	social cohesion & efficiency	efficiency & social cohesion

The Anglo-Saxon model

The UK undertook reform of its labour market in the 1980s, moving from the continental to what is known as the Anglo-Saxon model. Its more liberal labour market has been credited with increasing labour market participation, employment and FDI.

Figure 5.4: Protests against foreign labour in France

The Nordic model

The Nordic model has a very extensive welfare system and a high degree of income equality. Nordic governments also pursue very active policies to ensure a high level of employment (see box).

The Swedish model

Sweden has one of the world's most comprehensive tax-based welfare systems. Among the more startling OECD (Organisation for Economic Co-operation and Development) statistics is that the average Swede takes seventeen weeks off work each year – mostly through a combination of holidays, sickness and parental leave. Despite this, labour productivity grew by an average annual rate of 2.5 per cent between 1994 and 2004 – higher even than the USA.

Sweden is characterised by its welfare-to-work programmes, ambitious retraining schemes, specific programmes to integrate the disabled into the labour market and a world-class education system, with one of largest proportions of high school graduates in the world. But this social model cannot explain the success of the last ten years.

The Swedes are clear about policy goals and methods to achieve them, accepting higher taxes, market regulations, a fiscal surplus and conservative monetary policy for high levels of employment and social security, and an excellent welfare state and public services.

To make this work, consecutive governments implemented tough social reforms and deregulated product markets to bring down inflation. The reason for Swedish success is not the policies it has adopted, but how it has adopted them.

Source: 'Swedes show a dour Europe the way to reform', Wolfgang Manchau, *The Financial Times*, 3 April 2006 (adaptation)

Summary

On completion of this chapter you have learnt that:

- labour markets may not work efficiently due to lack of information, dominant buyers and sellers, under-provision of training and geographical and occupational immobility

- currently most unemployment in the EU is structural in nature

- unemployment is currently high in Poland, Slovakia and Greece, but low in the UK, Austria and Ireland

- productivity growth has been higher in the US than the EU, largely because of more investment in ICT equipment

- a flexible labour market can lead to high output and employment, but puts more pressure on workers to be adaptable and can create insecurity

- the EU has encouraged member countries to protect workers' rights – for example, in terms of the maximum hours they can work

- minimum wages are currently highest, in proportionate terms, in Malta and Ireland

- migration within the EU is limited because of geographical and occupational immobility of labour and restrictions placed on the movement of workers from new members

- the Continental labour market model is the least flexible of the main EU models.

Further reading

Baldwin, R., Wyplosz, C., Chapter 17 in *The Economics of European Integration*, McGraw-Hill, 2004

Grant, S., Vidler, C., Sections 4.6 and 6.6 in *Heinemann Economics A2 for AQA*, Heinemann, 2003

Grant, S., Vidler, C., Sections 4.9, 4.13 and 6.9 in *Heinemann Economics for OCR*, Heinemann, 2003

Useful websites

Employment and social policy: www.europa.eu.int/comm/employment_social/az_en.htm

Activities

Topics for investigation

Using up-to-date information from the Internet, newspapers and *The Economist* magazine, compare the performance of the French and UK labour markets.

Exam-style practice questions

Data response question
Polish plumbers

Workers from Eastern Europe are filling a range of vacancies in the UK, from cleaners to dentists. They are mainly coming from Poland. Differences in the structure and performances of the Polish and UK economies (see Table 5.4) is likely to see this migration continue for some time.

Table 5.4: Selected labour market data for Poland and the UK, 2003

	Poland	UK
Unemployment rate	18.0%	5.2%
Average wage	£4 956	£26 989
Net migration per 1,000	-0.3	2.1
Population change per year	-24 000	200 000
Population aged 15–64	70.7%	66.1%

Most economists believe the entry of eastern European workers into the UK economy is a success, keeping down inflation and promoting economic growth.

In contrast to the UK, France has been less welcoming to workers from the NMS8. In 2005 it gave only 875 work permits to Polish workers and in 2004 placed a ban on the free movement of workers from the new member countries. It was, in part, concerned that the impact of people coming into the country seeking employment may increase the number of French people without jobs. Such a view, assumes an unchanging demand for labour.

1. Using Table 5.4, compare the labour market in Poland and the UK.(5)

2. Analyse why 'the entry of eastern European workers into the UK' may:

    a) keep inflation down   (6)

    b) promote economic growth.   (6)

3. Discuss whether more migrant workers entering France would increase French unemployment.   (8)

Essay questions

1. a) Explain what is meant by labour market failure.   (10)

    b) Discuss the extent of labour market failure in the EU.   (15)

2. a) Explain what is meant by a flexible labour market.   (10)

    b) Discuss the costs and benefits to workers of a flexible labour market.   (15)

6 Farming in the EU

In this chapter you will learn:

- why agriculture is often protected
- why the prices of agricultural products, if left to market forces, tend to fluctuate and fall over time
- how a price system is designed to work
- why the CAP was reformed
- the key features of reforms to the CAP
- how farming varies across the EU
- what are the strengths and weaknesses of the CAP.

> **Key words** allocative inefficiency • buffer stock • CAP
> cobweb theory • government failure • minimum price
> multifunctionality • positive externalities • price support
> productive inefficiency • Single Payment Scheme
> strategic industry

Introduction

Farming accounts for a relatively small and declining proportion of EU output, income and employment. Indeed in 2005 it contributed only 1.6 per cent of the EU's output and accounted for about 10 million EU jobs (5 per cent of its employment).

The sector does, nevertheless, receive a considerable amount of economic, political and media attention. This is because the way EU farms are run and the support they receive has important consequences for the EU budget and for farmers, consumers and the environment, both inside and outside the EU.

Intervention in farming

In the EU what farmers produce, how they produce it and the prices they sell it for are influenced not only by market forces, but also by national government agricultural policies and by the **Common Agricultural Policy** (CAP).

Government intervention in agriculture is common throughout the world. Indeed agriculture is one of the most protected industries, with a high level of state intervention being found not only in the EU but also in, for instance, Japan, Switzerland and the USA.

Why are national governments and the EU so keen to protect and so preserve their agricultural sectors? There are a number of reasons. One is because agriculture is viewed as a **strategic industry**. Traditionally governments have wanted to ensure a relatively high and continuous domestic supply of food for fear that war, foreign blockades or disasters elsewhere could cut off the supply of imported food. Agriculture is also seen as a significant consumer of goods and services. The industry purchases a wide range of products including machinery, chemicals and insurance. A strong agricultural sector, therefore, is often seen as underpinning strong secondary and tertiary sectors.

In recent years, another factor has been influencing the level and form of intervention in the EU. This is the increasing recognition of the role agriculture has to play in supporting rural communities and in protecting the natural environment.

Although declining in number, farmers in the EU, particularly French farmers, also continue to form powerful political groups, which lobby both their national governments and the European Council for support.

The aims of the CAP

In the negotiations that led to the foundation of what became the European Union, France insisted on a system of agricultural support as its price for free trade in manufactured goods. The CAP started in 1962 when a mechanism was set up to subsidise farms through **price support**. It became fully operational in 1967. Its aims, stated in the 1957 Treaty of Rome, are:

- to stabilise agricultural markets
- to raise agricultural productivity (by promoting technical progress and by ensuring the rational development of agricultural production)
- to ensure a fair standard of living for the agricultural community, in particular by increasing the individual earnings of people employed in agriculture
- to assure the availability of supplies so as to make the area self-sufficient in agricultural products
- to ensure reasonable prices for consumers.

France persuaded the original members of the EU that it was desirable to both support agriculture and adopt a common approach to that support. With memories of the Second World War, and its disruption to the movement of food supplies still fresh in their minds, the member countries did not want to risk relying on imports of food. To ensure that their farmers would produce sufficient food, they thought it was necessary to introduce measures that would prevent the prices, and hence income, that their farmers received from fluctuating too much and to make those prices attractive.

Price movements

Agricultural markets are particularly vulnerable to price fluctuations. Many agricultural products have inelastic demand and inelastic supply. This means that any change in demand or supply has more of an impact on price than on quantity. Agricultural products can be subject to sudden and large changes in demand and supply. For instance, an outbreak of bird flu could cause a significant decrease in demand for chicken, and a drought could result in a large decrease in the supply of a range of agricultural products. Figure 6.1 shows the effect of a good harvest on the market for apples.

Price fluctuations can also arise due to the time lag between planning agricultural production and selling the produce. The **cobweb theory** (so-called because of the appearance of the diagram) suggests that price can fluctuate around the equilibrium for some time, or even move away from the equilibrium. In Figure 6.2, sheep farmers base their production decisions on the price prevailing in the previous time period. With P price of lamb, farmers produce Q quantity. This price produces a surplus, which

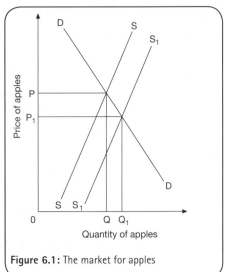

Figure 6.1: The market for apples

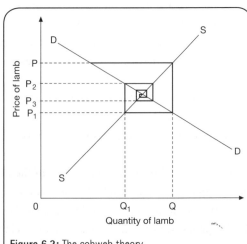

Figure 6.2: The cobweb theory

is sold at P_1. Based on this price, next season they supply Q_1 lamb, leading to greater demand than supply, so the price is driven to P_2. The next season the same process drives the price down to P_3.

Price fluctuations can drive some farmers, who would make a profit in the long run out of the industry and discourage other farmers from entering the industry. Farmers may also leave the industry as a result of the tendency for the price of agricultural products to fall, especially relative to manufactured goods. This is because demand does not tend to increase at the same rate as supply. Demand for most agricultural products is income inelastic, so that demand rises relatively slowly. In contrast, with a more scientific approach to farming and the greater use of machinery, the supply of agricultural products increases relatively rapidly.

The price support system

The CAP is not, and never was, a uniform system across the different agricultural products. There are a number of schemes or regimes operating, offering different levels and types of support. For instance, the main regime in the case of goat and sheep meat has always been a system of Private Storage Aid (PSA). This involves providing farmers with a partial subsidy to store the produce at times of oversupply – effectively to operate a **buffer stock.**

Up to 1992, however, the main feature of the CAP was the price support system designed to protect EU farmers from price fluctuations and, to a certain extent, foreign competition. This system, which continues in a modified form for a range of products including beef, cereals and rice, is based on three prices – a target price, a threshold price and an intervention price. The target price is based on the price that producers would need to cover their costs, including a profit mark up in the highest cost area. Its purpose is to act as a guide by which to calculate the threshold and intervention prices.

The threshold price is then set at a target price, minus the transport and handling costs for imported products. Imports are prevented from entering the EU below this threshold price by means of variable tariffs.

The intervention price is set below the target and threshold prices. Initially it was set at between 6 to 10 per cent below the target price. It acts as a **minimum price** or price floor which the EU guarantees to domestic farmers. If the market price is above the intervention price, farmers will sell their produce on the open market. If it falls below the intervention price, intervention agencies of the CAP will take one or both of two options. They may buy up the surplus supply and then store it or destroy it. Alternatively, or in addition, they may provide an export subsidy (also called a refund) to enable EU farmers to sell their produce relatively cheaply abroad. This compensates EU farmers for the difference in price they receive for exporting their produce and the EU intervention price.

When the CAP started the EU was a net importer of food. It was hoped that the policy would encourage EU production, reduce imports and move the area towards self-sufficiency. Figure 6.3 shows EU production of cereals rising from a to b and imports falling from af to cd.

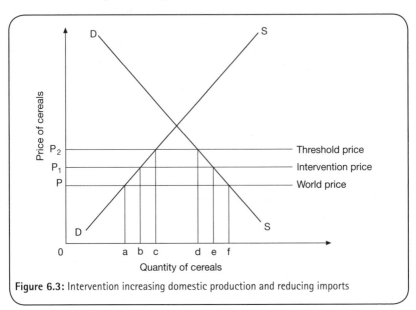

Figure 6.3: Intervention increasing domestic production and reducing imports

The price system soon proved to be rather too successful in encouraging EU production. The supply of a number of EU agricultural products increased significantly due to the relatively high intervention prices, which were often set not only above world, but also above the EU domestic market level. Indeed in a number of products, supply soon came to exceed demand as shown in Figure 6.4.

Assessment of the price support system

The greater security that a guaranteed price gave to farmers increased investment and, by being set above the market price, raised production.

By increasing EU output above the self-sufficiency level, however, a number of problems were created. The interventionist agencies of the CAP had to buy up a considerable amount of produce. These purchases plus the cost of storage and export refunds took up a considerable amount of the EU budget.

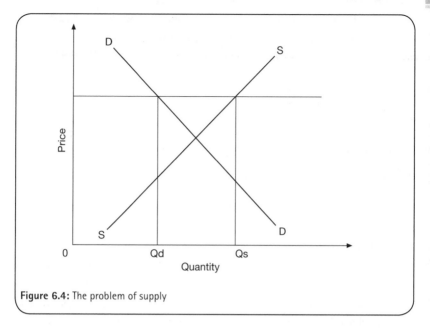

Figure 6.4: The problem of supply

EU consumers had to pay above world prices for most of the food they bought, thus reducing their consumer surplus.

Non-EU farmers were also penalised. They suffered a triple disadvantage, as it became more difficult for them to sell to the EU because of the tariff, and more difficult to sell both at home and to other non-EU countries because of EU export subsidies.

The price system also led to **allocative inefficiency** within and outside the EU. Farmers in the EU based their production decisions largely on which products received the most support, and not on what consumers wanted. In world terms there was also a misallocation of resources. Output in a range of agricultural products was below the allocatively efficient level in a number of non-EU countries which had the comparative advantage, and above the allocatively efficient level in EU countries. Providing a guaranteed price also encouraged a certain amount of productive inefficiency. Farmers did not face the same degree of market pressure to keep their costs low.

In addition, the price support system discouraged diversification, encouraged intensive farming and as a result caused environmental damage. The high CAP payments for some arable products, for instance oil seed, led to many farms being devoted to one crop, which is known as monoculture.

Price support linked to production further harmed the environment and animal welfare in a number of ways. Farmers sought to increase output by intensive use of fertilisers and pesticides and by making use of marginal land, which would not have been farmed at market prices. They also increased their stocking densities, engaged to a greater extent in factory farming and, in some cases, fed animals processed food containing carcasses of dead livestock.

Reasons for reform of the CAP

Over time the pressure to reform the CAP, particularly the price support system, built up. It became more unpopular with EU consumers who were paying both higher prices and higher taxes. Politicians were particularly concerned about the regressive nature of the policy. Higher food prices fall more heavily on the poor as they spend a higher proportion of their income on food.

Operating the CAP also became more expensive to operate for the EU. It was first thought that revenue from tariffs on imported agricultural products would be sufficient to cover CAP expenditure. By 1968, however, CAP expenditure had overtaken CAP tariff revenue. This net expenditure grew, and within a relatively short period was accounting for more than 70 per cent of the EU budget.

Growing wheat, beef and butter mountains in the 1980s and early 1990s meant the European Council became concerned that the long-term structural surpluses would see expenditure levels rising further. (See Figure 6.5 on the beef and butter mountains.) This concern became more intense towards the end of the 1990s, as the time approached for the entry of ten new member states, some with relatively large and inefficient agricultural sectors.

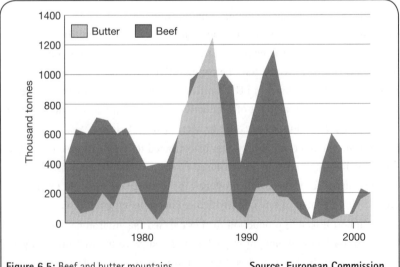

Figure 6.5: Beef and butter mountains   **Source: European Commission**

Over time, concern also built up about the environmental effects of the CAP. Intensive farming was seen to lead to a range of problems including soil degradation, pollution, depletion of water resources and diseases in livestock.

The UK was, and is, one of the main member countries pressing for reform of the CAP. This, in part, reflects that the UK is a net contributor to the CAP while, for instance, France is a net beneficiary – see Figure 6.6.

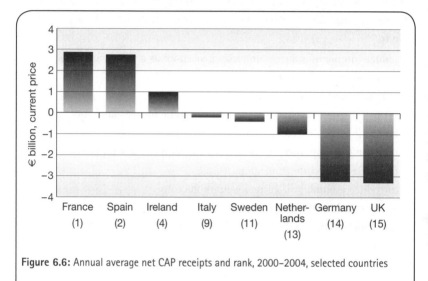

Figure 6.6: Annual average net CAP receipts and rank, 2000–2004, selected countries

Source: Calculations based on European Commission data; based on share in financing EU budget prior to budgetary corrections

As well as internal pressure there has, and continues to be, external pressure for reform. This has mainly been channelled through the World Trade Organization (WTO). The Cairns group (a group of food-exporting countries including, for example, Argentina, Australia, Brazil, the Philippines, New Zealand and South Africa), as well as Canada and the USA, have complained on a number of occasions to the WTO that the EU is dumping agricultural products in their markets while preventing access to EU markets. At the Uruguay Round meeting the EU acknowledged that the CAP was still protectionist, bureaucratic and that support was insufficiently decoupled from production. The agreement that was drawn up at the meeting committed signatories to liberalise their agricultural markets further in the future. The more recent Doha round of negotiations is putting further pressure on the EU to reform the CAP.

Recent reforms

From its inception, there have been a number of piecemeal reforms of the CAP. For example, in the 1980s milk quotas and set aside schemes were introduced and some limits were placed on price support, in an attempt to limit production. Since the 1990s there have also been four major reforms: the 1992 MacSharry reforms, the 1999 Fischler reforms, the Agenda 2000 reforms and the 2003 Fischler reforms. The major features of these reforms were to:

- reduce intervention prices and use them more as a safety net, rather than to stimulate production
- eliminate some intervention prices
- introduce grants for farmers who devote some of their land for environmental or recreational use
- increase the proportion of funds used for regional development
- decouple production from support
- introduce a number of animal welfare measures
- compensate for the early retirement of farmers aged over 55 years
- put a limit on CAP expenditure, fixing it in real terms at €40 billion until 2013
- switch from price support to direct subsidies.

The change in emphasis and approach implemented in these reforms was outlined in the new set of objectives outlined in Agenda 2000. These include constructing a competitive and safe agricultural system maintaining rural communities and the environment with clear definitions of which decisions belong at EU level, and which with individual states.

From 2005, the major way that the CAP has been supporting farmers has been through the **Single Payment Scheme** (SPS), also sometimes referred to as the Single Farm Payment (SFP). This combines and replaces a number of former direct payments. Farmers now receive one major payment. It is no longer based on production, but is determined on the basis of how much land is farmed, and on payments that were received in the years 2000–2002 (known as the reference years). To receive the payment in full, farmers have to meet a number of statutory environmental, food safety, animal welfare and safety at work standards. This requirement is known as cross compliance.

A further review of the CAP is expected in 2008 or 2009. This will probably further reduce intervention prices and export subsidies, especially as the WTO is committed to ending all export subsidies by 2013. Further reform of the dairy sector is also planned for after 2014.

Effects of the reforms

The two key effects of the reforms have been to change the CAP from a largely production-related scheme to a system of income support for farmers, and to widen the role of farmers.

The reforms have to some extent reduced intensive farming and surpluses. By lowering, or in some cases eliminating, intervention prices and decoupling payments from production, the gap between demand and supply has been reduced.

Figure 6.7 shows oversupply being reduced from ad to bc. In some cases, for example beef, overproduction has been eliminated to the extent that the EU has been turned into a net importer.

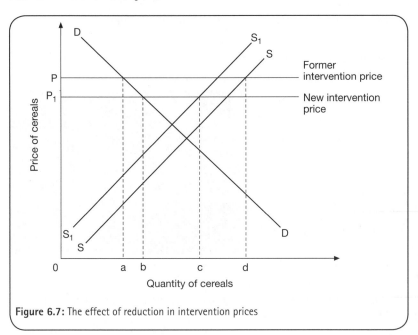

Figure 6.7: The effect of reduction in intervention prices

The reforms have exposed farmers to market forces to a greater degree. Indeed, it has been suggested that farmers are now basing their production decisions more on what consumers are demanding.

By reducing intervention buying, the reforms have reduced CAP expenditure as a percentage of the EU's budget. It still remains the biggest single item of expenditure, but by 2005 its share had fallen to 36 per cent.

The reforms have also placed more emphasis on the environment and on rural society. It is interesting to note that the original CAP aims did not mention the environment. Now farmers can receive payments for restoring hedgerows, opening up public access and for long-term set aside. They can also be paid for diversifying into other activities in a way that promotes rural development. The EU now sees farmers not just as producers of food, but also as managers of the environment and guardians of rural, cultural and social traditions. This idea that farming can fulfil a number of functions is referred to as **multifunctionality**.

Diversity within CAP

How many farmers there are and the contribution agriculture makes to a country's output varies across the EU. For example, in 2005 agriculture accounted for 5 per cent of Sweden's GDP, but only contributed 0.6 per cent to Sweden's GDP. Table 6.1 shows a number of the differences that exist between the farming sectors of the UK, France and Poland.

Within the EU, the support farmers receive depends on what they produce, the size of their farms and in which country they produce it. For example arable crops, beef and milk production receive more support than fruit and vegetables.

Generally farmers in the north receive more support than farmers in the south of the EU. This is not only because of what they produce, but also because of the size and efficiency of their farms. On average, farms are larger and more efficient in the north than in the south. For example,

Figure 6.8: Peasant farming in Poland

Table 6.1: A comparison between the agricultural sectors of the UK, France and Poland in 2004

	UK	France	Poland
Population	60.4m	60.7m	38.6m
Land area	244 820sq km	547 030sq km	312 685sq km
Agricultural land	16m hectares	28m hectares	16m hectares
Yield per hectare	7.5 tonnes	7.8 tonnes	–
Number of farmers	230 000	680 000	2 178 000
Labour force in agriculture	1.5%	4.1%	17.0%
% of GDP from agriculture	1.0%	2.7%	2.9%
Land prices	relatively high	relatively low	low

farms on the Parisian plan and in East Anglia tend to be both large and to use high-technology machinery, whereas farms in Greece tend to be smaller and use relatively basic agricultural equipment.

Farmers' experience is also influenced by how CAP policies are implemented in their country. The CAP allows a degree of discretion in how policies are operated.

Government failure and agriculture

Does the CAP increase or reduce efficiency in EU agriculture? The answer to this question is influenced by the extent that market failure would exist in the absence of intervention and how successful that intervention is.

The so-called European model of agriculture sees agriculture as capable of generating positive externalities in the form of maintaining rural communities and preserving the traditional appearance of the countryside, then output may be below the allocatively efficient level if it had been left to market forces. Figure 6.8 shows marginal social benefit (MSB) exceeding marginal private benefit (MPB) and, as a result, output of agricultural produce

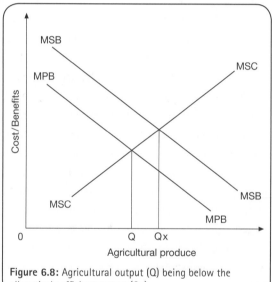

Figure 6.8: Agricultural output (Q) being below the allocatively efficient output (Qx)

being too low. It is likely, at current world market prices, that production and the number of farms would fall.

Intervention may also be justified on the grounds of health. Consumers may lack information about what certain foods contain, whether they meet the necessary standards and the effects of consuming particular agricultural products. However, it is surprising that the EU continues to subsidise tobacco production.

A case can be made that there is a relatively high degree of **government failure** in the policies of the CAP and how they are implemented. Some economists and politicians argue the cost of the CAP is too high. While as a proportion of the EU budget, the cost has fallen, it is still an expensive policy. It is also complex, with farmers having to work with regulations and forms.

On its original aims it may be claimed the CAP has stabilised agricultural markets to an extent. It has raised productivity, in large part by promoting technical progress, and as we have seen, been too successful in assuring the availability of supplies.

It is more debatable whether the CAP has ensured 'reasonable prices' for consumers and a 'fair standard of living' for farmers. Note that these terms are vague. EU consumers have actually faced relatively high prices and the CAP has had a somewhat inequitable impact within and between member countries. The regressive nature of higher food prices adversely affects the poor within a country. In the UK the richest 10 per cent of households spend 8 per cent of their disposable income on food, but the poorest 10 per cent spend 16 per cent on food. In rich member states spending on foods accounts for less than 15 per cent of disposable income, whereas in some of the poorer members it accounts for more than 30 per cent.

Average farm incomes have not risen in line with average incomes. This average figure hides a wide variation – from agribusiness, to part-time farmers. The CAP particularly benefits rich farmers, with approximately 80 per cent of CAP funds actually going to just 20 per cent of EU farmers. It is small EU farmers who have been leaving the industry at the rate of 2 per cent a year.

Efficient farmers in non-EU countries have also been driven out of business by the CAP's policies of domestic protection and export subsidies. By antagonising food exporting countries, the CAP threatens the EU's export markets in other products in which it does have a comparative advantage, such as software and biotechnology. Nevertheless, it has to be remembered that the EU is the world's largest importer of agricultural products, and some non-EU countries may benefit from being able to import cheap food from the EU.

By placing more emphasis on agriculture's wider role and opening up the industry to more competitive pressures at home and abroad, recent reforms have the potential to make EU agriculture more efficient. There is, however, the need for further debate on the role of agriculture and the extent to which it should be protected.

Summary

On completion of this chapter, you have learnt that:

- agriculture is viewed as a strategic industry
- the initial aims of the CAP were to stabilise agricultural markets, raise agricultural productivity, increase farm income, and to ensure availability of supplies and reasonable prices for consumers

- if left to market forces, agricultural prices tend to be unstable and to fall over time
- initially the main policy measure of the CAP was price support
- setting a minimum price can result in oversupply and the high costs of intervention buying and storage
- pressure for reform came from within the EU (due to high prices, high costs and concern about environmental effects) and forces outside (where the CAP is seen as unfair competition)
- key features of recent reforms include decoupling production from support, and increasing the role of farmers
- both market and government failure can occur in agriculture.

Further reading

Baldwin R., Wyplosz, C., Chapter 8 in *The Economics of European Integration,* McGraw-Hill, 2004

Grant, S., Vidler, C., Section 4.8 in *Heinemann Economics A2 for AQA,* Heinemann, 2003

Grant, S., Vidler, C., Section 6.11 in *Heinemann Economics for OCR,* Heinemann, 2003

Useful websites

Europa: www.europa.eu.int/com/agriculture/intr/index_en.htm

Activities

Topics for investigation

Using the website mentioned, find out how recent reforms have affected the market for beef in the EU.

Exam-style practice questions

Data response question

Most of the world's 800 million olive trees grow by the Mediterranean Sea; each tree can yield about six quart bottles of olive oil each year. However, olive oil is a case study that shows how rich-country subsidies make it hard for farmers in poor countries to earn a living. Morocco, Tunisia, Lebanon, Syria and Turkey are the lowest cost producers, but 95 per cent of the olive oil sold in world supermarkets comes from Spain, Italy and Greece. This is because the EU neutralises the advantage through paying European olive oil growers US$2.3 billion a year.

If Arab, Israeli or Turkish oil producers can still compete, they also face tariffs of €1.2 or €1.3 per kilo of oil if they hope to sell in Europe. Therefore, despite 260 factories producing 290 000 tons a year, Morocco's olive oil exports for 1997 peaked at 35 000. By contrast, Andalusian growers a few miles north export half a million tons a year. Despite US imports of olive oil doubling since 1996, Arab-world producers have felt no benefit – only 3 000 tons of 215 000 imported by the USA came from the Arab world, compared to 215 000 from the EU. Not all money from the EU though gets to the farmers – a recent Spanish investigation revealed eleven individuals had applied for and received US$750 000 in subsidies, despite not being connected to the business.

Source: 'European olive oil subsidies are twice the value of world olive oil trade', www.ppionline.org_ci.cfm

1. Which countries appear to have the comparative advantage in olive oil production? Explain your answer. (3)

2. What evidence is there in the extract above of government failure? (4)

3. Explain two possible reasons why the EU subsidises the production of olive oil. (8)

4. Discuss how production subsidies and tariffs can distort trade. (10)

Essay questions

1. The New Zealand government has reduced the amount of support it gives its agricultural industry.

   a) Explain how a government may support its agricultural industry. (10)

   b) Discuss the arguments for reducing such support. (15)

2. a) Explain why prices for agricultural products tend to be unstable. (10)

   b) Discuss whether setting a minimum price for agricultural products always reduces economic efficiency. (15)

7 The EU, trade and the global economy

In this chapter you will learn:

- why trade is central to the internal and external affairs of the EU
- why the principle of comparative advantage has some relevance in explaining the EU's current pattern of trade
- what is meant by trade creation and trade diversion in a customs union such as the EU
- how, through trade, the EU's member states are heavily dependent on each other
- why the EU is the most powerful economic bloc in the world economy
- about the EU's links with NAFTA and developing countries
- what is meant by globalisation and how it has come about
- how globalisation has impacted on the economic affairs of EU member states.

> **Key words** common external tariff • comparative advantage customs union • de-industrialisation • foreign direct investment globalisation • global sourcing • multinational corporations trade creation • trade diversion • unit labour costs

Introduction

The ongoing development of trade between member states is the central aim of the EU's trade policy. This was the underpinning economic principle that was set down in the 1957 Treaty of Rome. It has also been the most important motive for geographical enlargement, as the current EU has grown from six to 25 members in 2004.

At the same time, an external trade policy has also developed within the context of the **customs union**. Again, the purpose has been for the benefit of member states, while providing the EU with those goods and raw materials that cannot be produced efficiently from within. This aspect of trade policy has been more controversial than internal trade policy, since it is in many respects protectionist. Despite this criticism, EU member states have a substantial presence in the trade pattern of many other countries and groups in the global economy.

Internal trade policy

Article 2 of the Treaty of Rome makes clear that the purpose of the European Union is to establish 'a common market'. This has been achieved through the elimination of customs duties and quantitative restrictions on the import and export of goods between member states. For the original six members, this was achieved by 1966, nine years on from the Treaty of Rome. As geographical enlargement has occurred, the customs union has been the first aspect of membership to be realised and, in terms of benefits, has applied to relatively poor as well as richer accessionaries.

Impact of a customs union on trade

In a customs union like the EU, where external tariffs tend to selectively restrict trade with non-members. The relevance for internal trade in the EU is that **trade creation** occurs. In this situation, once trade barriers are removed, a certain amount of consumer spending switches from a higher-cost supplier within a member state to a lower-cost supplier from within the EU. As a result intra-EU trade will increase (see Table 7.1).

In the case of the UK, for example, with the EU25, it is now cheaper for retailers to buy television sets, clothing and other products from lower-cost suppliers in the Czech Republic, Hungary and Poland. In turn, a Czech manufacturer of cars may find it cheaper to purchase vehicle parts from (say) Germany, where manufacturers are more price competitive due to the benefits of economies of scale. In both examples, domestic manufacturers lose out; but consumers gain an increase in welfare through a more efficient allocation of resources and lower prices.

A second effect of the customs union is that of **trade diversion.** This is a situation where previously consumers purchased products at a lower price from producers anywhere in the world. The combination of imposing a tariff on imports into the customs union, and removing barriers to trade between member states, makes many imports more expensive. In other words, lower cost supplies from outside the EU are replaced by higher cost supplies from within.

For the UK especially this has been a major issue, particularly in the case of agricultural products and food items. Prior to joining the EU, the UK imported vast quantities of these items from Canada, Australia and New Zealand. Today, fruit, meat, dairy products and cereals from these countries have virtually disappeared from the shelves of UK supermarkets. In their place are similar products from Spain, France, and Italy and, increasingly, Poland. This diversion of supplies, leading to higher costs to consumers, invariably results in a loss of consumer welfare. It also impacts on non-EU producers and is particularly serious where these producers are from developing economies that are heavily reliant upon this type of trade.

Figure 7.1 shows this effect in theoretical terms. Prior to joining the customs union, the average world price for food products was P_w. At this price, domestic demand was at Q_{dd} and a small amount, Q_{ds}, was supplied by domestic producers. On joining the customs union, the **common external tariff** (CET) on food products raises the price that has to be paid by domestic consumers to P_t. This results in a fall in domestic demand, depending on the price elasticity of demand, and an increase in supply from previously higher cost producers from within the customs union. Although there is revenue from the tariff, the main welfare issue is a loss of consumer welfare, as represented by the two deadweight loss triangles.

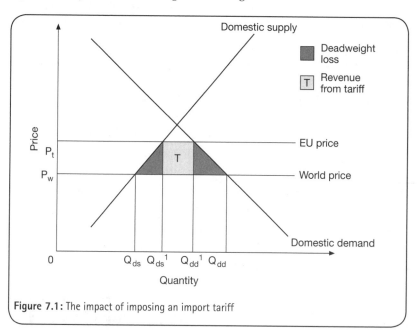

Figure 7.1: The impact of imposing an import tariff

Effect of a customs union

It follows from the above that the overall effect of a customs union depends on the relative strength of trade creation and trade diversion. Most studies indicate very clearly that the gain in consumer welfare from annual trade creation greatly exceeds the loss in consumer welfare from trade diversion. For the customs union as a whole, most show a net benefit of around four to five times the loss due to trade diversion. However, for individual member states this is very dependent on the general pattern of their trade.

UK loosing £35 billion a year to EU

Britain's membership of the EU is costing more than £35 billion a year, according to new research by Patrick Minford and his team at Cardiff Business School. This loss is because the UK has to pay artificially high prices for imported foods and goods, compared to prices on the world market. This cost is caused by the protective barriers erected by the EU, including tariffs on goods imported from outside the EU.

Minford claims the UK would gain 2.5 to 3.5 per cent of GDP a year if the UK left the EU. EU policies raise the price of many manufactured goods by some 30 to 80 per cent above world price levels.

Source: *The Business* 5 September 2004 (adaptation)

The growth of economic dependency

Over the years, various empirical studies have attempted to assess the effects of free trade among member states. The message from all is very clear, namely that intra-EU trade has developed substantially. Figure 7.2 shows that it has grown at a faster rate than the EU's external trade, in particular since 1985. This growth has been way beyond the most optimistic forecasts made by economists at the time the EU was established. Up to the 2004 enlargement, intra-EU trade has also consistently grown at a faster rate than world trade. There have been particular instances of growth following the

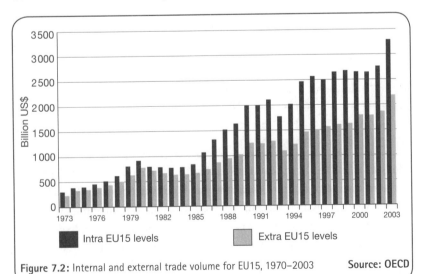

Figure 7.2: Internal and external trade volume for EU15, 1970–2003   **Source: OECD**

admission of new member states, although there has been some variation in the experience of individual countries.

The growth in intra-EU trade has in turn furthered the dependence of the economies of member states on each other. This can be demonstrated crudely in Table 7.1 which shows thee following.

- Almost 62 per cent of exports and over 60 per cent of imports of EU15 members were from within.
- For the countries shown, there are substantial variations in their degree of dependence.
- The smaller southern European economies of Spain and Portugal have trade patterns that are heavily concentrated on trade with fellow member states. Although not indicated in Table 7.1, other smaller economies such as Ireland, Austria, Belgium and Denmark also rely very heavily on trade with the rest of EU15.

In the case of the UK less than 30 per cent of exports and imports of goods were with EU members at the time of entry in 1973. This percentage has almost doubled as progressively, UK businesses have been able to trade freely and more competitively in those goods where they have a relative advantage. It must not be forgotten, though, that the UK had a deficit or over £25bn on its trade in goods with the rest of the EU in 2003 (see Figure 7.3).

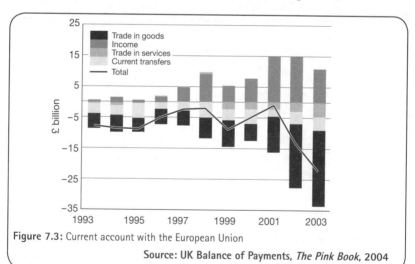

Figure 7.3: Current account with the European Union

Source: UK Balance of Payments, *The Pink Book*, 2004

Table 7.1: Export and import shares in the EU trade in goods for selected member states in 2002

Exports to (%)

	EU15	France	Germany	UK	Spain	Portugal
EU15	61.8	61.4	54.5	58.8	71.6	80.7
USA	9.3	7.8	10.5	15.0	4.4	5.6
Japan	1.6	1.6	1.9	1.9	0.8	0.3
Canada	0.9	0.8	0.9	1.7	0.5	0.5
Acceding countries	4.8	3.2	8.2	2.3	3.1	1.3
Candidate countries	1.5	1.4	1.8	1.0	1.4	0.6
CIS	1.6	1.0	2.5	0.7	0.8	0.2
OPEC	2.4	3.9	2.0	2.8	2.5	0.7
Other emerging markets	9.1	11.7	9.8	10.0	8.9	6.8
Asia	5.6	5.2	6.9	6.9	2.9	1.6
Latin America	1.5	2.4	1.4	1.1	3.2	1.0
Africa	2.0	4.1	1.5	2.0	2.8	4.1
	100	100	100	100	100	100

Imports from (%)

	EU15	France	Germany	UK	Spain	Portugal
EU15	60.4	66.1	55.2	52.6	67.3	77.9
USA	7.0	6.8	6.3	12.0	3.4	2.1
Japan	2.7	1.9	3.1	3.6	1.9	1.7
Canada	0.6	0.6	0.5	1.5	0.3	0.2
Acceding countries	4.3	2.1	9.9	2.1	1.6	1.8
Candidate countries	1.4	1.2	1.9	1.4	1.1	0.8
CIS	2.4	1.8	3.0	1.3	2.1	1.1
OPEC	2.3	2.9	0.9	1.1	5.7	3.6
Other emerging markets	12.5	10.8	11.4	17.4	12.4	7.7
Asia	8.6	5.9	9.1	12.3	6.5	3.1
Latin America	1.8	1.9	1.2	1.9	2.9	2.7
Africa	2.1	3.0	1.2	3.2	3.0	1.9
	100	100	100	100	100	100

Source: Economic Forecasts, Spring 2004, European Commission

How can comparative advantage be recognised?

Since joining the EU, the UK economy has experienced major structural change. Some of this change has been as a consequence of competitive pressures from within the EU. More recently, structural change has been the result of pressures arising from **globalisation**. Irrespective of the cause, the result has been the following.

- **De-industrialisation** has been extensive. Entire industries have closed down, while in others there has been considerable rationalisation and concentration of ownership, as firms have sought to remain competitive. In 2004, manufacturing contributed less than 20 per cent of GDP.

Table 7.2: UK balance of trade in selected goods only, 1994/2004 (£ million)

Product group	Balance of trade	
	1994	2004
Food beverages and tobacco	-3 849	-11 601
Crude oil and oil products	3 937	1 869
Semi-manufactured goods	380	-3 743
of which chemicals	4 650	4 087
Finished manufactured goods	-8 151	-41 277
of which motor cars	-3 534	-6 636
other consumer goods	-5 208	-19 307
Total trade in goods	**-11 126**	**-58 614**

Source: UK Balance of Payments, *The Pink Book*, 2004

- Increasingly, the UK is being seen as a provider of research and development activity. These services are exports, and in many cases support manufacturing activity in countries with lower **unit labour costs**, some of which are in the rest of the EU25.

UK balance of trade

Table 7.2 shows the UK's balance of trade for selected goods over the period 1994 to 2004. At first glance the UK would appear to have lost much of its relative advantage to countries that have developed their own comparative advantage through the manufacture of goods being produced where unit labour costs are low. For clothing, textiles, electrical goods, toys and so on this is clearly true.

However, there is similar evidence that shows the UK can maintain a competitive position. This is particularly true of chemicals, especially pharmaceutical products. Also in 2004, the UK was a net exporter of oil, although the net balance of this trade was falling. In other specialised fields of manufacturing, UK businesses have maintained a competitive edge, a point not clear in Table 7.2 due to the crude levels of aggregation used.

In 2004, the UK was the second largest exporter of services in the world economy. Trade in services with the USA was very firmly in credit, while dealings with the EU25 were more finely balanced. It was fortunate that trading deficits could be offset by this other type of trade balance.

Taking the EU25 in 2004, there was great variability in the trade balances of member states. For example:

- the UK had by far the largest deficit
- in contrast, Germany had an estimated surplus of around €140 billion
- Ireland and the Netherlands had respectable surpluses of €38 billion and €30 billion respectively
- all of the new NMS8 applicant countries had deficits, the largest being that of Poland at around €7.8bn.

External trade policy

The EU as a power in world trade

Article 3 of the Treaty of Rome stated that the EU will establish a common customs tariff and 'a common commercial policy towards third countries'. The former, or CET as it is usually known, has two main functions, as listed below.

- To protect the interests of member states by seeking to ensure that certain activities are not subject to unfair competition from low cost providers elsewhere, while providing member states with products the EU is unable to produce itself. For example, the maximum CET is particularly high, up to around 230 per cent, on agricultural and food products that the EU can produce for itself. Although much lower at 13 to 17 per cent, it is highly protective for clothing and footwear products. Overall, in 2004 the average agricultural products CET tariff was 16 per cent, and just 4 per cent on non-agricultural products.
- To ensure that all member states within the customs union apply the same CET as each other on trade in particular products with particular trading partners.

The wider common commercial (trade) policy objectives have been applied through multinational, regional and bilateral approaches. The EU is one of the key players in the World Trade Organization (WTO) and has been a driving force behind the latest round of negotiations, such as the Doha Development Agenda that has sought to reduce trade barriers with developing economies to help them combat poverty. The EU has a long history of offering preferences to the African, Caribbean and Pacific (ACP) group of countries. Bilateral approaches have covered sensitive agricultural products such as sugar, bananas, rice and textile products from China.

UK loses out in bra wars fiasco

The 'bra wars' fiasco, in which 80 million sweaters, bras, trousers and other clothing were blocked in European ports, highlights how EU measures can damage the UK's best interests. The 1974 protectionist Multi-Fibre Agreement (MFA) limited clothes imports, benefiting EU manufacturers and employees, but at a high cost to customers.

The 1994 agreement with the World Trade Organization to phase out the MFA by 2004, allowed a transition period for manufacturers to adapt. While some have, others, notably in France, Italy and Spain, continue to produce low cost items. These are now very vulnerable to Chinese competition.

Capitulating to pressure from these countries, Peter Mandelson, the EC's trade commissioner, signed a two and half year deal with China to restrict clothing imports. The 'bra wars' arose, as this led to goods that had been ordered by UK retailers before the quota deal being blocked in harbours.

Again, the UK loses out because it cannot negotiate unilateral trade deals. Retailers and consumers lose money. In the 'bra wars', the free traders have been the clear losers.

Source: *Daily Telegraph*, 12 September 2005 (adaptation)

Pattern of EU international trade

The EU is the largest trading power in the world. In 2004 the EU25 was responsible for 18 per cent of all world merchandise exports and imports, excluding intra-EU trade. The USA had 11.9 per cent of world exports, but 18 per cent of world imports. Particularly the USA, but also the EU, had deficits in this type of trade. In contrast China, with 9.1 per cent of world exports and 7.2 per cent of imports, had a massive surplus, as indeed did Japan, which was the fourth largest force in world merchandise trade in 2004. The incorporation of the NMS8 countries into the EU was in part responsible for a widening deficit in 2004.

Figure 7.5 shows the composition of the EU's trade in goods in 2004. The USA, China, Switzerland, Russia and Japan are the EU's main trading partners from an export and import standpoint. They are closely followed by Norway and significantly, from a political standpoint, Turkey. Overall, other developed industrialised economies account for over half the EU's total trade. The balance of trade differs from country to country. In recent years, the EU has had trade surpluses with its new NMS8 partners, the USA and Canada. This contrasts with a widening deficit with China (over €78 billion in 2004) and regular deficits with Japan and other Asian tiger economies.

In terms of products, as might be expected, the EU is a major importer of oil, gas and other energy products. Imports of quality tobacco and a range of foodstuffs that the EU cannot grow for itself exceed exports of European agricultural products. At the same time, exports of manufactured products have continued to grow at a steady rate, mainly in line with growth in the world economy as a whole. This has been particularly true of chemicals,

The major EU import partners

Rank	Partners	Mio euro	%
	World	1 027 580	100.0
1	USA	157 386	15.3
2	China	126 712	12.3
3	Russia	80 538	7.8
4	Japan	73 505	7.2
5	Switzerland	61 398	6.0

The major EU export partners

Rank	Partners	Mio euro	%
	World	962 305	100.0
1	USA	233 803	24.3
2	Switzerland	74 957	7.8
3	China	48 033	5.0
4	Russia	45 662	4.7
5	Japan	43 053	4.5

EU imports of goods

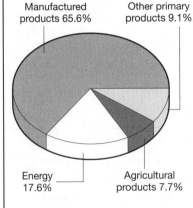

Manufactured products 65.6%

Other primary products 9.1%

Energy 17.6%

Agricultural products 7.7%

EU exports of goods

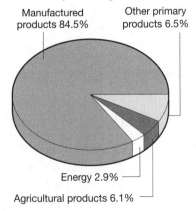

Manufactured products 84.5%

Other primary products 6.5%

Energy 2.9%

Agricultural products 6.1%

Figure 7.4: EU trade in goods by major partners and sectors in 2004

Source: Eurostat (Comext)

transport vehicles and equipment and certain types of industrial machinery where the EU retains a comparative advantage.

Trade with other world trading units

The EU25 is the largest and most integrated economic bloc in the world economy. Elsewhere, there are other units with looser forms of organisation. In the main, these have involved the removal of internal trade restrictions between members, but without the restriction of a CET. The world's largest free trade area is the North American Free Trade Association (NAFTA), which was launched in 1994 when its three members, the USA, Canada and Mexico, agreed to progressively reduce tariff barriers between themselves. Members are free to negotiate external trade relationships on a bilateral basis.

Other free trade units in the world are as follows.

- Latin America, which currently has 20 members in South and Central America.
- European Free Trade Association (EFTA). The four remaining members – Switzerland, Norway, Leichtenstein and Iceland – have tariff-free trade for imports of manufactured goods into the EU.
- Association of South East Asian Nations (ASEAN) with ten members, all of which are emerging industrial economies.

As Tables 7.3 and 7.4 show that links with NAFTA are particularly substantial, given that the USA is the EU's principal trade partner. Trade between the EU25 and NAFTA could well be adversely affected in the future as the euro emerges as a strong world currency in international markets. This could influence the trade in goods as well as the flows of **foreign direct investment** (FDI) and stocks between the two organisations.

Table 7.3: EU trade with other world trading units, 2004

	EU imports from (m€)	EU exports to (m€)	EU imports and exports (m€)
World	1 029 326 (100%)	963 709 (100%)	1 993 035 (100%)
NAFTA	17.6 %	28.1 %	22.7%
Latin America	5.5 %	5.0 %	5.2%
EFTA	11.7%	11.3%	11.5%
ASEAN	6.7%	4.4%	5.6%

Source: Eurostat (DG Trade)

Table 7.4: Balance of EU trade with NAFTA by product, 2004 (m€)

Agricultural products	+ 4 084
Energy	+ 8 613
Machinery	+ 12 008
Transport equipment	+ 20 090
Chemicals	+ 19 496
Textiles and clothing	+ 4 407

Source: Eurostat (DG Trade)

Trade policy with developing countries

In relative terms, the world's least developed countries (LDCs) seem to be at a disadvantage when it comes to trading with the EU. As the principle of **comparative advantage** indicates, this need not necessarily be the case. In 2003, the EU imported 58 per cent of all its world imports from LDCs, including 61 per cent of all agricultural imports. By way of comparison, the figures for the USA were 32 per cent of all imports, and just 14 per cent of agricultural imports.

Over the years, the EU has given preferential access into its market for a range of agricultural products, raw materials and a limited range of manufactured goods from the ACP group of countries. This agreement, under various Lomé Conventions, has also provided special forms of aid and technical assistance. Typical products included are cocoa, coffee, bananas, wood, iron ore, sisal, cotton, rubber and tea. Most of these are products the EU is unable to produce for itself. Another feature of the conventions is that the EU does not require preferential access for its own exports into ACP markets, leaving countries free to get the best deal available on world markets.

Superficially, this might seem to have been a good arrangement for the ACP countries. However, there are various criticisms that could be made.

- Despite preferential access, the export performance of the ACP group has been disappointing (see Table 7.5). Their market share in EU trade is small and has been declining.
- Developing countries outside of the ACP group such as India, Bangladesh, Pakistan, and many countries in North Africa and Central America, are not given preferential access. This has increasingly been seen as discriminatory by the WTO. Matters came to a head in 1999 with the so-called 'banana wars' (see box).

Table 7.5: EU trade with the ACP countries,[1] 2004

Product group	% Imports Into EU	% Share of total EU imports	% Exports from EU	% Share of total EU exports
Mineral fuels	26.4	4.1	5.6	5.3
Food & live animals	24.4	13.3	10.8	8.5
Manufactured goods	16.7	4.4	11.7	2.5
Crude materials	11.9	8.0	1.6	2.5
Machinery & transport equipment	8.6	0.7	45.0	2.7
Beverages & tobacco	2.4	12.1	2.6	4.6
Other	8.3	2.0[2]	20.5	2.0[2]
	100	2.8	100	2.7

[1] excludes South Africa
[2] estimates

Source: Eurostat (DG Trade)

Going bananas

The 'banana wars' have been ongoing since the 1990s. The US claims that the EU gives an unfair advantage to banana imports from its former colonies discriminating against Latin American producers. American companies, such as Chiquita and Del Monte, control production in Latin American countries. In 1999 the USA announced a new 100 per cent import tax on a range of European products. Heated negotiations led to the EU introducing a new set of tariffs by 1 January 2006.

Autunm 2005 saw the latest round in the conflict. The EU planned to abolish quotas on Latin American imports, but increase the duty. The present rates are 2.7 million tonnes a year with a duty of €75 per tonne, rising to €680 per tonne when the quota is reached. The EU proposed fixing the duty at €230 per tonne. ACP nation imports would remain duty free. The WTO supported the Latin Americans, who have a 60 per cent market share in the UK, compared to 20 per cent for ACP producers.

Globalisation and the EU

Globalisation is the process of growing interdependence between the economies and businesses in the world at the present time. In a simple form, it is evidenced through the wide range of goods that can be purchased and that are available in almost any economy. Typical examples of global brands are Microsoft Windows, Coca-Cola, Big Mac, Nescafé instant coffee, Kellogg's Corn Flakes, Cadbury's Dairy Milk, Land Rover and so on. These brands invariably come from **multinational corporations** such as Nestlé, IBM, Sony, Panasonic, Ford, Nike and so on. The list is constantly growing, and includes European, as well as US and South East Asian companies.

The growth in world trade has been a major driving force in promoting globalisation. Here of course the EU has played its part in the international community by reducing protectionist measures and barriers to trade, particularly with developing and emerging economies, as seen earlier in this

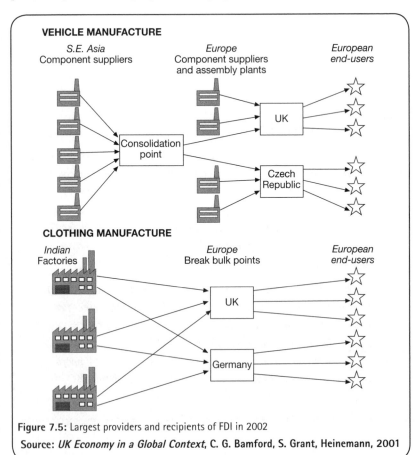

Figure 7.5: Largest providers and recipients of FDI in 2002

Source: *UK Economy in a Global Context*, C. G. Bamford, S. Grant, Heinemann, 2001

chapter. Underlying this growth in world trade has been increased **global sourcing**, the term used to describe the way in which manufacturers and retailers in developed economies, such as the EU, source their businesses worldwide. Figure 7.5 shows two typical diagrammatic representations of global supply chains.

Foreign direct investment

Another very important feature of globalisation has been the spectacular growth in flows of FDI. This term is used to describe the acquisition by residents of a country of real assets abroad. Inward FDI is when, for example, US and Japanese companies purchase businesses and other assets in another country. It can be measured as a stock (over a period of time) or as a flow (on an annual basis). FDI can bring major economic benefits to an economy. These include employment creation, stimulating competition, technology and skills transfer and innovation.

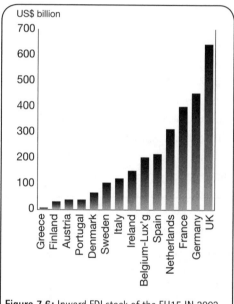

Figure 7.6: Inward FDI stock of the EU15 IN 2002
Source: UNCTAD

Within the EU, as Figure 7.6 makes clear, by the end of 2002 the UK had received more FDI than any other member state. This is in many respects a remarkable achievement given the UK's geographical detachment from the rest of the EU. It is a very positive indication that foreign companies see the UK as a good market in which to base their operations and from where they can produce goods for the EU market as a whole.

The UK's perspective

The UK's position, though, should be seen in perspective. The following two points can be made.

- By the end of 2003, inward FDI stock for the UK was just short of 40 per cent of GDP. In Ireland, it was about 130 per cent of GDP, by far the highest figure of any EU member state, and of major significance in Ireland's economic advance. Of the NMS8 economies, Hungary (55 per cent of GDP) and the Czech Republic (48 per cent of GDP) have been important beneficiaries. In both cases, FDI has increased to these levels from a virtually nil base in the early 1990s.

- Outward flows of FDI should also be taken into account. In 2002, the UK was the world's second largest investor after the USA. In net terms, for the UK, the stock of outward FDI by UK businesses was around US$1 050 billion, compared to inward FDI of around US$650 billion.

The global economic power of the US cannot be ignored. It is sometimes said that 'when the USA sneezes, the whole world catches a cold'. In terms of FDI, the USA is largest provider as well as the largest recipient (see Figure 7.7). In many respects the EU appears to have fallen behind the USA in terms of its ability to attract inward investment. It is believed that higher labour costs, skills deficiencies and a restrictive regulatory environment for business are some of the factors that have deterred companies from investing in the EU. Although not entirely borne out by the data, the negative attitude to EMU and the single currency might also account for the recent reluctance of US and Japanese investors to increase their investments in the UK.

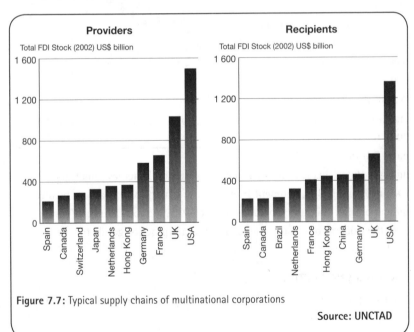

Figure 7.7: Typical supply chains of multinational corporations

Source: UNCTAD

Globalisation: the challenge and opportunities for the EU

In 2005, the Treasury produced an important report on the long-term global economic challenges and opportunities for Europe. A summary is shown in the box. This followed an earlier White Paper from the Dti on 'Making globalisation a force for good'. A key theme of this report was that the EU must ensure that the Doha round of international trade negotiations provided a fairer deal for developing economies that will enable them to share in the benefits of globalisation.

Long-term global economic challenges and opportunities for Europe

This report was produced to coincide with the UK's presidency of the EU in the second half of 2005.

Six global challenges were identified.

- *The EU in the future will account for a diminishing share of world output with the rise of India and China.*
- *The EU must attract more FDI.*
- *The continuing drain of European service sector jobs to emerging economies for example, call centres, banking jobs, word processing and data input.*
- *The need for Europe to be more innovative and more responsive to technological change.*
- *The need for European labour markets to be more flexible.*
- *To meet the increased demand for energy that is associated with increased growth.*

The way forward is for Europe to meet the challenges of the global economy through:

- *having a stable macroeconomic environment*
- *providing the right climate for enterprise and innovation*
- *ensuring the competitive Single European Market reaches its full potential*
- *being more outward looking*
- *having modern social policies*
- *ensuring enhanced sustainability in the use of energy resources.*

Source: HM Treasury, 2005 (adaptation)

The UK government believes that the EU has a crucial role to play, given its importance as the world's largest economic bloc. This role should involve:

- reducing current barriers to trade with the USA and developing economies
- controversially, reforming the CAP by cutting out subsidies that harm the agricultural interests of developing economies
- completing the liberalisation of internal product, capital and labour markets.

The White Paper also recognised that the international community has to work together to ensure that all developed economies reduce trade barriers for products where developing countries have a comparative advantage. This is a huge challenge, given the protectionist attitude of the US and the attitude of some EU countries with respect to the CAP. The UK's view is that it is only through such relaxation that the benefits of globalisation can be shared by all of the world's economies.

Summary

On completion of this chapter, you have learnt:

- that the growth of intra-EU trade has produced substantial benefits for all member states and has made them more integrated and dependent on each other
- the principle of comparative advantage can be used to explain the current pattern of trade of member states and of the EU as a whole
- that the EU is the world's largest, and in certain respects, most powerful economic bloc in the global economy
- why inward and outward FDI is an important feature of the global economy
- why the benefits of globalisation have been far from equally distributed
- how the EU should be striving to get a better deal for the world's poorest countries within the global economy.

Further reading

Grant, S., Vidler, C., Section 6.20 to 6.22 in *Heinemann Economics A2 for AQA*, Heinemann, 2003

Grant, S., Vidler, C., Section 5.12, 5.13 and 5.20 in *Heinemann Economics for OCR*, Heinemann, 2003

Smith, D., Chapter 9 in *Current Economic Policy* (3rd edition), Heinemann, 2003

Useful websites

HM Treasury: www.hm-treasury.gov.uk

Europa: www.europa.eu.int/comm/trade/issues

Activities

Topics for investigation

Obtain data on the pattern of trade for an EU15 member state of your choice. Analyse this information to identify product groups where there is possible comparative advantage. Repeat this for one of the NMS8 countries and comment on any differences that you observe.

Exam-style practice questions

Data response question

The letters that follow are adapted from *Daily Telegraph* on 3 March 2006 in response to an earlier article on the relative merits of cane and beet sugar. Read them, then answer the questions that follow.

SIR – As Europe's main cane sugar refiner Tate & Lyle acts as the most important bridge to Europe for African, Caribbean, Pacific and least developed countries.

This access is independent of EU market demand, but commands an EU price, giving suppliers between £250 million and £300 million more for their sugar than would otherwise be the case. Last year this meant that 300 000 direct employees in some of the world's poorer economies benefited from additional income for their raw sugar, compared with what they would have received by selling in the world market, competing with producers such as Brazil, Australia and Thailand. These funds are vital to sustaining their economies and employment.

Robert Gibber
Tate & Lyle
London EC3

SIR – Your article indulged in the nation's favourite pastime – farmer bashing. Yes, beet pulp from refining is used for animal feed, but what is wrong with that? It ensures there is no waste and it is not a 'foul smelling mass', just innocuous, sweet smelling shreds.

Beet farming does not have a 'corrosive effect' on the soil; it has its place in the crop rotation and uses no more pesticides than other crops. Subsidies help with the higher cost of European production. Most cane sugar is grown on large farms in South America, subsidised by very low wages, long working hours and a disregard for health and safety conditions, not just by small farmers seeking fair trade.

Beet sugar is produced, refined and consumed in this country, so demands no unnecessary food miles – something you have applauded in previous articles.

Helen Bletcher
Appleby, Lincs.

1. Using diagrams, show:

   a) how the EU pays above the world market price for cane sugar from ACP countries   (5)

   b) the effects of subsidy on the market for beet sugar in the EU.   (5)

In each case, write a few sentences of elaboration.

2. Using the information in the Tate & Lyle letter, explain how the multiplier process can be used to analyse the effects of the increased income that is paid to sugar cane farmers.   (6)

3. Comment on the relative sustainability of cane and beet sugar production   (9)

Essay questions

1. a) Explain the principles of absolute and comparative advantage.   (10)

   b) Discuss the extent to which these principles can be applied to explain the current pattern of EU trade.   (15)

2. a) Explain what is meant by globalisation.   (10)

   b) Comment upon the view that 'globalisation benefits the few developed economies and provides few, if any, benefits for the world's least developed economies'.   (15)

Examination skills for The European Union

Synoptic assessment

The economics of Europe features heavily in the present A level specifications, especially those from OCR and AQA, where there are specific so-called 'synoptic' papers at the A2 stage. These are as follows.

- **OCR. 'Economics in a European Context.'** This examination consists of a small number of questions drawn from stimulus material that is pre-circulated a few weeks before the examination.
- **AQA. 'Economics of the European Union.'** In this examination, students are required to write a report on a particular EU issue, such as unemployment, regional policy, the euro, economic blocs and so on. Various items, such as extracts from reports and data sets, are provided and advice is given on the structure that the report should take.
- **Edexcel. EU topics** such as EMU, the CAP and international trade are included in the subject content of 'The UK in the global economy' synoptic unit.

OCR and Edexcel examination questions follow a conventional format. The emphasis of tasks in all synoptic papers is on an evaluation of the issues involved.

It is important that you fully understand what is meant by 'synoptic'. The easiest way of seeing it is that, in your answers, you need to be able to draw on the full range of skills and economic concepts that you have studied in your A level course. If you can do this, then you are seeing the connections involved and beginning to think as an economist. Europe is the *context* for the application of the concepts you have learnt and for the various skills you have developed.

We have endeavoured to follow this approach in this book by avoiding unnecessary factual detail while concentrating on the economic concepts involved. So, from an examination perspective:

- use economic concepts and terminology in your answers whenever you can
- avoid reproducing great volumes of information from the pre-circulated material (OCR) or that provided as the basis of the examination (AQA)

- where you are using data, do not regurgitate what has been provided – analyse trends, pick out the main features, and so on
- remember that to score high marks, your answers (and aspects of your AQA report) must include some evaluation of the issues involved.

General principles

When sitting any examination, it is important to remember the basic skills that are needed for success.

So, remember to do the following.

- **Allocate your time effectively** in relation to the marks available. In the case of the OCR examination, you need to spend at least 30 minutes on the last question; for AQA, around 25 minutes should be left for the final recommendations in your report. Edexcel's question paper has two sections – spend around 45 minutes on each and, for each section, carefully note the marks available, allocating writing time accordingly.
- **Write to the point of the question or task.** Avoid writing material that is superfluous to the question or task. A diagram can sometimes be a helpful way developing an answer ... provided you can draw it correctly! And as stated earlier, use economic terminology as much as you can.
- **Construct your answer in a way that is consistent with the 'directive' word in the question.** This is very important in these synoptic examinations – a high grade can only be obtained where your answers include appropriate evaluation. Below are three typical directive words to look for.
  - 'Discuss' – this word is inviting you to look at two sides of an argument, putting forward the case for and the case against. A very good answer should conclude with an overall statement as to which is most acceptable.
  - 'Comment' – this word is inviting you to give a reasoned opinion, not necessarily in the form of the cases for and against. Your comment will have more meaning if it is underpinned by appropriate evidence.
  - 'Evaluate' – this word is asking you not only to look at both sides of an argument but also to weight your views in some way. This could simply be by saying that one side of the argument carries more weight that the other, for instance. It is similar to 'discuss' except that some final assessment is required.

Two other common directive words are as follows.

  - 'Analyse' – this requires you to set out the main points in an argument while avoiding detail. It can often be a signal for you to include a diagram in your answer.

- 'Examine' – this is used a lot in Edexcel question papers and can be interpreted in the same way as 'analyse'.

Types of questions

Two main types of questions are asked.

- **Essay-type questions** require answers to be written in continuous prose. (OCR and Edexcel synoptic units. For AQA, the report should be assembled in continuous prose, possibly including a few bullet points where appropriate.)
- **Data response-type questions**, where some interpretation of the numerical information provided is required. (OCR's synoptic unit usually starts with a simple question involving the interpretation of data; the AQA stimulus material usually includes blocks of data that have to be interpreted as part of the report writing process.)

Essay-type questions

In synoptic examinations, although the style of essay question may vary, the nature of the requirement is that examiners are looking for answers that are clearly written, follow a logical structure and, above all, contain relevant economic concepts and ideas that fit together in a coherent way. This is not as daunting as it may seem ... provided you give careful thought before you start writing as to how your answer should be laid out. You should also remember what was said above about directive words.

A typical essay question might be:

'Discuss whether the UK should join the EU's single currency.' (AQA, June 2002, adaptation)

A simple structure would be:

First paragraph   Two or three contextual sentences. For example, 12 EU member states signed up from 2002. The UK did not and has adopted a 'wait and see' attitude. You could also mention the 'Five Tests'. 'When' rather than 'if' seems to be the preferred attitude.

Body of answer   A series of points as set out in Chapter 3, in particular in the box 'The Great EMU Debate – is the UK better "in" or "out"? Your answer should be a balanced one, with an equal volume of analysis for and against membership of the euro.

You also need to make a very important point – membership of the euro also brings with it the ECB's common interest rate and implications for the UK's domestic economy and the way in which the economy can be managed.

Conclusion   Make the point that there are arguments for and against, as set out in the body of your answer. You could conclude by saying that any decision on membership will have to be taken from a political as well as economic standpoint.

A few more tips are:

- remember to use Economics terminology as much as you can
- refer to things you have read, or to arguments put forward by well-known authorities on the topic
- if drawing on stimulus material or extracts, make reference to it, for example, 'as Extract 2 states' or 'as the data in Extract D indicates'.

Data response-type questions

Data is widely used in AQA's and OCR's synoptic units. Irrespective of the question or the way in which you are required to use the data, it is important you understand what the data means. Four simple stages should be followed.

1. Pick out any relevant economic terms in the table or chart headings.
2. Make sure you know what the data means. Look at the units (if any) and whether the data is in raw, percentage or index form.
3. Spend time 'eye balling' the data. Look along rows or down columns to pick out trends. Make sure you are clear if it is cross-sectional or time series data.
4. Look for the source and see if you have come across it in your studies. AQA students are advised to spend around 20 minutes at the start of the examination to become familiar with the extract material. Use this time to try to do these four stages for each set of data provided. OCR students can take more time. The general principles above, though, still apply.

Worked examples of typical examination questions

Question 1

Comment on whether both the European Commission and the competition authorities in member states should be concerned about the growing market power of grocery retailers.   (15 marks) (OCR, Unit 2888, January 2006)

(Note: The context for this question is an extract on the growing market concentration of grocery retailers in the EU15 member states and summarises two reports by the UK's Competition Commission and Office of Fair Trading, clearing the major supermarkets of 'ripping off' customers and applying unfair practices in their dealings with suppliers).

Advice on what is required

From a synoptic standpoint, this question requires you to draw on your knowledge of:

- how prices are determined, and why concentration of power in a market can lead to market failure
- more specifically, how firms behave in monopolistic and oligopolistic markets and why, in such cases, there may not be an efficient allocation of resources
- what criteria need to be evidenced for there to be intervention by competition authorities.

A good answer to this question should be underpinned by relevant economic analysis such as:

- a comparison of the market equilibrium of monopoly and that of a competitive market (this could include a diagram; the inefficient nature of monopoly should be clearly made).
- how firms compete in oligopolistic markets, making reference to price rigidity, branding and (possibly) collusion
- how this affects both supermarket consumers and their suppliers
- why, under certain circumstances, monopolies and oligopolies may not be as anti-competitive as made out by the theory. For example, benefits from economies of scale, product innovation and development.

A very good answer must focus on the 'comment' directive word of the question. Possible comments could include:

- the problem of compiling evidence of the anti-competitive behaviour of powerful grocery retailers
- the fact that two UK inquiries have in the main cleared supermarkets of anti-competitive behaviour
- the reasons for intervention by the European Commission, compared to that of competition authorities in member states.

A couple of paragraphs focusing on one or two of these issues should result in a very good mark being awarded.

As this outline worked example has identified, the skill in synoptic examinations it to focus on the economic concepts, keeping the contextual material to a modest amount.

Question 2

Extract 1

Excise duty on tobacco products in selected EU member states (2000)

	Excise duty per packet of 20 cigarettes (€)	Revenue from excise duty on tobacco products (€bn)	GDP (€ bn)	Revenue from excise duty on tobacco products as % GDP
Greece	1.14	1.71	117	1.46
Ireland	2.93	0.85	85	1.00
Spain	0.97	4.06	559	0.73
Sweden	2.05	0.71	224	0.32
UK	4.21	5.69	1 351	0.42

Note: This table contains the excise revenues on all tobacco products: cigarettes, cigars, cigarillos and smoking tobacco. VAT is not included in the figures.

Using Extract 1, compare the taxation of tobacco products in the UK with that in Spain and Ireland.   (6 marks) (OCR, Unit 288, June 2005)

Advice on what is required

'Eye balling' the data should indicate that:

■ the first column refers to cigarettes, the second and fourth columns refer to all tobacco products
■ the fourth column of figures is derived by dividing the second column of figures by column 3 x 100%
■ in the UK, cigarettes are much more heavily taxed than in the other four member states; they are taxed least in Spain
■ the UK government receives the largest absolute revenue from taxing tobacco products
■ the % GDP raised from taxing tobacco products is very variable.

Once these basics have been established, let us consider the question. 'Compare' is often used as a directive word in data response questions. It simply means 'look at what is similar and look at what is different'. Here, it requires you to compare the UK, on the one hand, with Spain and Ireland. (You will also note that some of the data is not needed, namely the data for Greece and Sweden and also the GDP column. This is quite normal.)

When interpreting data, it is very useful to quantify any variations you might observe. For example, the UK excise duty on cigarettes is greater than in either Spain or Ireland. It is €1.28 greater (44.7%) than in Ireland and €3.24 (334%) greater than in Spain. You will get additional marks if you refer to the mathematical extent of differences.

Other variations you might observe can be drawn from the second and fourth columns of figures using the same principle as used above. For instance:

- the UK receives the highest aggregate excise duty from tobacco products, Ireland the least
- the UK receives a lower percentage of its GDP from excise duty on tobacco products than do Spain or Ireland.

In both cases a quantification of the differences will earn you more marks than if you just make general statements.

Conclusion

Over time, the EU has widened and deepened. Its greater width has resulted from an increase in membership. The greater depth has come from increased integration. What of the future? How many members will the EU have in 20 years time and how integrated will it be?

Countries will still want to join the EU if they believe membership will strengthen their economies. Ireland and Spain have seen their economic performance transformed since membership. The extent to which their higher GDP per capita and lower unemployment rates are attributable to EU membership is, of course, debatable. Nevertheless, most economists agree that membership has been one factor behind their success. The experience of new members will depend both on how they respond to the opportunities and challenges of membership and on how the EU as a whole performs.

In its early years, the EU grew more rapidly than the USA. Now it is growing more slowly than the USA and has higher unemployment. This relatively poor performance has increased the debate about the need to reform some of the EU's policies and about the desirability of future integration. The main area that the UK is pressing to reform is the Common Agricultural Policy. Reforms to labour markets and social policy are also under discussion. The eurozone is one area which is about to change with the imminant adoption of the single currency by the NMS.

These NMS are committed to joining the single currency. To reap the full benefits of using the euro, it is crucial that new entrants' economies converge with the current members. The NMS are already well integrated in terms of their trade with the eurozone. What is more questionable is whether the one-size-fits-all interest rate will benefit them. Currently their economies are still relatively divergent from the members of the eurozone. Even those economies which have been in the eurozone since 1999 are not converging to the extent anticipated.

With some members using the same currency, a European Central Bank, a high level of intra-EU trade and a single market, there is already a relatively high degree of integration within the EU. How much more integration should there be? While the French and German governments, for instance, favour more integration of policies, the UK government is more cautious.

In an increasingly globalised market, there will be more pressure on the members of the EU to be competitive and dynamic. Their chance of achieving this would be strengthened by being part of a strong EU. But what is the best way forward for the EU?

Index

ACP countries 25, 101, 104–5
acquis communautaire 10, 13
administration 17, 25
age discrimination 69
agriculture 13, 15, 24, 78–9, 80–1
   see also CAP
airlines 37, 43, 44, 57
anti-trust measures 58

Bamford, C.G. 36
banana wars 104, 105
budget, EU 6, 23–6, 46, 84, 87
Bulgaria 18–19

CAP (Common Agricultural Policy) 11,
   25, 78, 87, 120
   aims of 79–80, 90
   allocative inefficiency 83
   diversity within 88–9
   and government failure 89–90, 91
   minimum prices 81–2, 91
   price support system 81–4
   reasons for reform 84–5
   recent reforms 86, 91
capital flows 12, 27, 40–1
car industry 14, 50–3, 55, 56
China 18, 101, 102
cohesion funds 24, 41, 42
common external tariff 3, 95, 100
comparative advantage 28, 99–100
competition policy 57–9, 60
competitiveness 18, 21, 24, 50–3
contributions to budget 24, 25
convergence 10, 27–8
criteria for joining 9–10, 27–8
   Copenhagen criteria 9–10, 12, 18

Croatia 18–19
customs union 3, 7, 93, 94–6

de Villepin, Dominique 73
Delors, Jacques 27, 48, 49
developing countries 104–5

economic blocs 2–3
economic growth 11, 15–16, 34, 54–5
economic and monetary union (EMU)
   3, 26–34
   convergence criteria 27
   costs of 30–3
   development of 26–8
   and UK 33–4, 46
economies of scale 11, 41, 50–2
EEA (European Economic Area) 3–4, 7
EFTA 2, 3, 7
employment protection 68–71, 75
enlargement 4, 20, 42
environment and CAP 85, 87
environmental policy 24, 42–5, 46
ERDF 36, 41, 42
EU15 4, 5, 13, 17–18, 98
   2003–2012 performance 16–17
EU25 2003–2012 performance 16–17
euro 13, 26–7
European Central Bank (ECB) 29–30
   role of 6, 7, 27
European Union
   aims and origins 1–2, 7
   groupings within 4–6
   membership 4–6
eurozone 4–5, 7, 14–15, 67–8, 120
   2003–2012 performance 16–17
   interest rate 29–30

exchange rates 14–15, 27, 28
expenditure of EU 24–5

fiscal sovereignty, loss of 31–2
foreign direct investment 11, 12, 34, 103, 106–8, 110
   and NMS 14, 21, 53–7
   providers and recipients 106, 108
France 26, 30–1, 32, 85, 88, 98, 120
   labour market 72–3
freight transport 35–9
funding 11, 12–13, 20, 41–2

GDP 16, 40
Germany 26, 30–1, 32, 98, 100, 120
   tin can tax 45
global warming 45
globalisation 48, 68, 99, 106–10
   role of EU 25, 110
Grant, S. 43
greenfield operations 50, 54
Griffiths, A. 58
grocery retailers 55, 56, 57

harmonisation: transport 37, 38

income, EU 24, 25
inflation 15–16, 29–30, 32–3
institutions of EU 6
integration 2–3, 10
interest rates 14–15, 27, 31, 120
   and EMU 29–30
Ireland 12, 17, 30, 31, 64, 120
   inward FDI 107–8
   trade 97, 100
Ison, S. 58

Japan 48–9, 78, 98, 101–2
joint ventures 54, 57

labour costs by country 56
labour market 62, 72–4, 75
   failure 62–3, 75
   flexibility 67–8, 75
   models 72–3, 74, 75
   participation 65
labour mobility 71–2, 75
labour and regional problem 40–1
liberalisation: transport 36–8, 39
Lisbon strategy 65
living standards 39–40, 54

Maastricht Treaty 9, 27
membership of EU 4–6, 7, 9, 20
   benefits of 10–11
   preparing for 11–13, 20
   see also enlargement; NMS
merger control 58
migration 17, 20, 71–2, 75
Minford, Patrick 96
minimum wages 67, 68–71, 73, 75
monetary policy 6, 7
monetary sovereignty, loss of 30–1
mutual recognition 37

NAFTA 2, 18, 103, 104
NMS (new member states) 4–5, 15, 120
   benefits of membership 11, 20
   characteristics of 13, 15–16, 21
   doing business in 53–7
   effects of entry 13–18
   NMS8 4, 9, 100, 102
non-tariff barriers 48, 49, 57, 60

performance, EU15 and NMS 15–19
Poland 15, 23, 26, 64, 88, 100
pollution 43–4, 85
portfolio investment and NMS 14

prices 28–30, 32–3, 80–4
    cobweb theory 80–1
    and intra-EU trade 94–5, 96
productivity growth 65–7, 75

rail freight 35, 36, 38–9
recycling 44, 45
regional aid 11, 15, 24
regional policy 39–42, 46
regional problem 39–41
road freight 35, 37, 38
Romania 18–19

service sector in NMS 50, 56–7
single currency 14–15, 20, 26–7, 120
    and price transparency 28–9
    see also euro
Single European Act (1986) 3, 27, 40
Single European Market 3, 48–53, 60
    benefits of 50–3
    completion of 36–9
    four freedoms 49–50
social funding 24, 41, 42
sovereignty, economic 14, 27, 30–2
Spain 17, 97, 98, 120
Stability and Growth Pact 15, 28,
    31–2
structural funding 41–2
Sweden 17, 26, 74, 88

taxes 24
    diesel fuel 38
    flat 18
TERFN 38–9
trade 11–12, 27, 101–5
    creation and diversion 14, 94, 95

and economic dependency 96–8
    intra-EU 94–5, 96
    policy 93, 94–101, 104–5
    removal of NTBs 48, 49, 50–7
transport policy 35–9, 46
Treaty of Rome (1957) 2, 35, 48, 79
    trade 93, 94, 100
Turkey 19–20, 21, 102

unemployment 15, 17, 34, 62, 63–5,
    73
    2003 eurozone 30–1
    2005 by country 65, 75
    cyclical 63, 64
    structural 64, 75
United Kingdom 66, 68–9, 85, 88, 120
    balance of trade 99–100
    car industry 52–3
    and EMU 33–4, 46
    FDI 107, 108
    and MFA 101
    and migration 17, 71–2
    rebate 23, 25–6
    and single currency 26
    trade 94–5, 96, 97
United States 2, 18, 72, 78, 108
    productivity 66–7
    trade 98, 100, 101, 103, 104

Vidler, C. 43

working hours and conditions 68–9
WTO 6, 18, 85, 86, 101, 104, 105